KU-259-279

BURNS IN HIS TIME

BURNS
in his time

ALAN DENT

with illustrations by Elizabeth Corsellis

STIRLING
DISTRICT
LIBRARY

NELSON

THOMAS NELSON AND SONS LTD
36 Park Street London W.1.
P.O. Box 336 Apapa Lagos
P.O. Box 25012 Nairobi

THOMAS NELSON (AUSTRALIA) LTD
597 Little Collins Street Melbourne

THOMAS NELSON & SONS (SOUTH AFRICA) (PROPRIETARY) LTD
P.O. Box 9881 Johannesburg

THOMAS NELSON AND SONS (CANADA) LTD
81 Curlew Drive Don Mills Ontario

THOMAS NELSON AND SONS
Copewood and Davis Streets Camden 3, N.J.

© Alan Dent 1966
First published 1966

821.6

DEN

Printed in Great Britain by
Thomas Nelson (Printers) Ltd, London and Edinburgh

CONTENTS

ACKNOWLEDGMENTS

The author and publishers thank the following publishers for permission to quote passages from the books named:

Hamish Hamilton, Ltd., for *Robert Burns* from *Nocturnes and Rhapsodies* by Alan Dent.

Macmillan & Co., for *Address to a Burns Club* from *Preludes and Studies* by Alan Dent.

ILLUSTRATIONS

TO MY DEAR BROTHER, JACKIE,

John Jeffrey Dent

MY ARMS ABOUT MY DEARIE O

1 · Yet Another?

YET another account of the life-history of the most overwritten and overpraised poet in the whole of world literature? This book is nothing of the sort. It is primarily an attempt to set Robert Burns in his period and to communicate the flavour and tang of that period. And it is secondarily a collection—formed throughout a lifetime—of the wisest and shrewdest and most eloquent appraisals which the poet met with in his lifetime and received after his death.

Both as historian and anthologist, I write as an Ayrshire-born critic (7th January, 1905, at Maybole, the ancient capital of Carrick and a bare seven miles from the bard's own birthplace at Alloway). It follows that I have the advantage of knowing the Burnsian countryside intimately and of loving it dearly. It follows, too, that I have the disadvantage of having been reared and educated, both in Ayrshire and in Glasgow, in a milieu where no poet other than Burns would be quoted or read or even countenanced. Not even any other Scottish poet! It is not a special argument—it is a plain matter of fact—that Scotland has

ANDREW LANG

shamefully neglected its other men of letters because it has been so shamelessly busy in adulating Burns for the two centuries and more of his existence. I would go so far as to opine that Burns himself would resent this—in the name of justice and good sense.

But an opening chapter is no place in which to lose one's critical temper. Let me instead quote one of those neglected Scots littérateurs on the subject. He is Andrew Lang (1844–1912), writing without spleen or prejudice or unfairness, in an introduction to yet another edition of the poems of Burns, in the year 1906, when I was one year old. Let me give no more than his opening paragraph:

'The life of Robert Burns has been written so often, the history of his career has been so intensely scrutinised, his poetry has passed under the eyes of critics so numerous and so distinguished, that to say about him what is both new and true is perhaps impossible. The discovery of fresh letters or other manuscripts may add to our information and our pleasure, but cannot alter our estimate of his character and his genius. Burns has suffered from the good offices of his apologists, who absolve him where he very frankly condemns himself. To say anything whatever about him, good or bad, is, and always has been, to lay un-hallowed hands on the Ark, and to provoke certain Scottish enthusiasts who talk much more about their national poet than they read him. These fanatics nobody can please, nor is it my intention to try to please them.'

That was the thing to say, and it is well said.

But others, more accomplished even than Andrew Lang in Scottish literature, have dared to criticise its godhead. And woe betide the Scottish writer who does not give absolutely uncurbed adulation to the expression of his regard for the National Poet! I have always felt—and the feeling is particu-larly strong in Edinburgh—that the permanent cloud under which two of Scotland's most eminent writers, Thomas Carlyle and Robert Louis Stevenson, stay obscured and therefore unscrutinised is due to their having dared to mix literary and moral criticism with their appreciation and assessment.

Take R.L.S. first. In the year 1876 the *Encyclopaedia Britannica* invited him to write a condensation of Burns's life and a criticism of his works. The editor found the essay too *critical* and 'too much at variance with the accepted Scottish tradition', and though payment was made for the essay it was not used. Stevenson replied on the 8th of June: 'I suppose you are per-fectly right in saying there was a want of enthusiasm about the article. To say truth, I had, I fancy, an exaggerated idea of the gravity of an encyclopaedia, and wished to give mere bones, and to make no statements that should seem even warm. And perhaps also I may have a little latent cynicism, which comes out when I am at work. I believe you are right in saying I had not said enough of what is highest and best in him. Such a topic is disheartening; the clay feet are easier dealt with than the golden head.' But to the overwhelming majority of the Scots —including presumably the then editor of the Encyclopaedia— this particular idol *has* no clay feet.

Stevenson was too experienced a journalist to waste copy, and it is probable—if not certain—that it was at least the substance of this article which appeared in 1879 in *The Cornhill Magazine* (October) under the title *Some Aspects of Robert Burns*. This essay appeared under the same title in Stevenson's volume of literary essays, *Familiar Studies of Men and Books,* three years later. Stevenson's view is the oddest mixture of fair and confused thinking. He writes what he thinks for a sentence or two, and then he writes what he thinks he ought to think for another sentence or two. Here is an example:

'It may be questionable whether any marriage could have tamed Burns; but it is at least certain that there was no hope for him in the marriage he contracted. He did right, but then he had done wrong before; it was one of those relations in life which it seems equally wrong to break or to perpetuate. He neither loved nor respected his wife. "God knows," he writes, "my choice was as random as blind man's buff." He consoles himself by the thought that he has acted kindly to her; that she has a good figure . . . The effect on the reader is one of un-mingled pity for both parties concerned. This was not the wife who (in his own words) could enter into his favourite studies or relish his favourite authors; this was not even a wife, after the affair of the marriage lines, in whom a husband could joy to place his trust. Let her manage a farm with sense, let her voice rise to B natural all day long, she would still be a peasant to her lettered lord, and an object of pity rather than of equal affection.'

All these fine sentiments and fine-spun sentences blink the fact—which R.L.S. *must* have known—that the wife in question, Jean Armour, had presented the poet with no fewer than four children—two sets of twins—before the pair started the experiment of wedlock.

R.L.S. continues:

'She could now be faithful, she could now be forgiving, she could now be generous even to a pathetic and touching degree; but coming from one who was unloved, and who had scarce shown herself worthy of the sentiment, these were all virtues thrown away, which could neither change her husband's heart nor affect the inherent destiny of their relation. From the outset it was a marriage that had no root in nature [for myself I should have said that it had a four-fold root!] and we find him, ere long, lyrically regretting Highland Mary, renewing correspondence with Clarinda [Mrs. McLehose in Edinburgh], on doubtful terms with Mrs. Riddell, and on terms unfortunately beyond any question with Anne Park.'

Let me again interrupt R.L.S.'s *tant soit peut* moralising to point out that Anne Park was a Dumfries barmaid who presented Burns with a daughter exactly nine days before Jean, now wedded as well as bedded, gave him another son. It is very much to Jean's credit — though R.L.S. does not bring it to our attention — that she adopted Anne Park's child and brought it

R . L . STEVENSON

up with her own. In this action—highly unusual in any woman in any age or circumstances—it has always seemed to me that Jean showed a very complete understanding of her remarkable husband's fundamental nature as well as a certain lack of grudge and temper unusual in her sex.

R.L.S. writes movingly, and with altogether sounder judgment, about the poet at the end of his tether and near the end of his days:

'He knew, knew bitterly, that the best was out of him; he refused to make another volume, for he felt that it would be a disappointment; he grew petulantly alive to criticism, unless he was sure it reached him from a friend. For his songs, he would take nothing; they were all that he could do; the proposed Scottish play, the proposed series of Scottish tales in verse, all had gone to water; and in a fling of pain and disappointment, which is surely noble with the nobility of a Viking, he would rather stoop to borrow than to accept money for these last and inadequate efforts of his muse.'

I would rather say 'noble with the nobility of a distinctly foolish Viking'. And Stevenson goes on in a way which suggests he secretly thought the same:

'And this desperate abnegation rises at times near to the height of madness; as when he pretended that he had not written, but only found and published his immortal *Auld Lang Syne*. In the same spirit he became more scrupulous as an artist; he was doing so little, he would fain do that little well; and about two months before his death he asked Thomson [the Edinburgh song-publisher] to send back all his manuscripts for revisal . . . The battle of his life was lost; in forlorn efforts to do well, in desperate submissions to evil, the last years flew by. His temper is dark and explosive, launching epigrams, quarrelling with his friends, jealous of young puppy officers. He tries to be a good father; he boasts himself a libertine. Sick, sad, and jaded, he can refuse no occasion of temporary pleasure, no opportunity to shine; and he who had once refused the invitations of lords and ladies is now whistled to the inn by any curious stranger . . . He

THOMAS CARLYLE

had trifled with life, and must pay the penalty. He had chosen to be Don Juan, he had grasped at temporary pleasures, and substantial happiness and solid industry had passed him by. He died of being Robert Burns, and there is no levity in such a statement of the case; for shall we not, one and all, deserve a similar epitaph?'

Thomas Carlyle dealt with Burns in a long essay which was really a review of Lockhart's *Life of Burns* and which appeared in *The Edinburgh Review* when its author was only thirty-three. Carlyle, unlike R.L.S., had the sense to avoid any moral judgments and so keeps himself free from the 'holier-than-thou' attitude. But, at the very end of his essay, he gives interesting reasons for his abstention:

'We had something to say on the public moral of Burns; but this also we must forbear. We are far from regarding him as guilty before the world, as guiltier than the average; nay, from doubting that he is less guilty than one of ten thousand. Tried at a tribunal far more rigid than that where the *Plebiscita* of common civic reputation are pronounced, he has seemed to us even there less worthy of blame than of pity and wonder. But the world is habitually unjust in its judgments of such men; unjust on many grounds, of which this one may be stated as the substance: it decides, like a court of law, by dead statutes; and not positively, but negatively, less on what is done right, than on what is or is not done wrong . . . Here lies the root of many a blind, cruel condemnation of Burnses, Swifts, Rousseaus, which one never listens to with approval. Granted, the ship comes into harbour with shrouds and tackle damaged; the pilot is blameworthy; he has not been all-wise and all-powerful: but to know *how* blameworthy, tell us first whether his voyage has been round the Globe, or only Ramsgate and the Isle of Dogs.'

And his conclusion, for Carlyle, is very pretty indeed and completed and rounded off with less than the usual tautology:

'With our readers in general, with men of right feeling anywhere, we are not required to plead for Burns. In pitying admiration he lies enshrined in all our hearts, in a far nobler mausoleum than that one of marble; neither will his Works, even as they are, pass away from the memory of men. While the Shakespeares and the Miltons roll on like mighty rivers through the country of Thought, bearing fleets of traffickers and assiduous pearl-fishers on their waves; this little Valclusa Fountain will also arrest our eye: for this also is of Nature's own and most cunning workmanship, bursts from the depths of the earth, with a full gushing current, into the light of day; and often will the traveller turn aside to drink of its clear waters, and muse among its rocks and pines!'

PAGE OF MS. OF TAM O' SHANTER

But Pleasures are like poppies spread,
You sieze the flower, its bloom is shed;
Or like the snow falls in the river,
A moment white, then melts for ever;
Or like the Borealis' race,
That flit ere you can point their place;
Or like the rainbow's lovely form,
Vanishing amid the storm:
Nae man can tether Time or Tide,
The hour approaches Tam maun ride;
That hour, o' Night's black arch the key-stane,
That dreary hour Tam mounts his beast in;
And sic a night he took the road in,
As ne'er poor sinner was abroad in. —

The wind blew as 'twould blawn its last,
The rattling showers rose on the blast,
The speedy gleams the darkness swallowed,
Loud, deep, & lang, the thunder bellowed:
That night, a child might understand
The deil had business on his hand. —

Weel mounted on his grey meare, Meg,

It is a very temperate estimate for a great Scot on a great Scot. But I think it is a just one.

Where Carlyle is less than just is in his odd estimate of some of the works, particularly of *Tam o'Shanter,* which I deem—as indeed most Burns readers deem—to be a spontaneous masterpiece of the highest order. Carlyle opined otherwise:

'It is not so much a poem, as a piece of sparkling rhetoric; the heart and body of the story still lies hard and dead. He has not gone back, much less carried us back, into that dark, earnest, wondering age, when the tradition was believed, and when it took its rise; he does not attempt, by any new modelling of his supernatural ware, to strike anew that deep mysterious chord of human nature, which once responded to such things; and which lives in us too, and will for ever live, though silent now, or vibrating with far other notes, and to far different issues . . . The piece does not properly cohere: the strange chasm which yawns in our incredulous imaginations between the Ayr publick-house and the gate of Tophet, is nowhere bridged over, nay, the idea of such a bridge is laughed at; and thus the Tragedy of the adventure becomes a mere drunken phantasmagoria, or many-coloured spectrum painted on ale-vapours, and the Farce alone has any reality. We do not say that Burns should have made much more of this tradition. [What else has the silly Sage been saying?] We rather think that, for strictly poetical purposes, not much *was* to be made of it. Neither are we blind to the deep, varied, genial power displayed in what he has actually accomplished; but we find far more "Shakespearian" qualities, as these of *Tam o'Shanter* have been fondly named, in many of his other pieces.' [I do not.]

And he concludes his helter-skelter prose-ride with a grudge with which we could hardly agree less, saying of the supernatural *Tam:* 'It might have been written, all but quite as well, by a man who, in place of genius, had only possessed talent.' The critical Carlyle was criticised in his turn by William Archer, another Scot, though one who could be thoroughly detached since he was a London dramatic critic for forty-five years. He deplored Carlyle's tone of patronage, apology and commiseration, and said well and wisely of the poet himself: 'In his own art, in the art of Scottish vernacular poetry, he did attain consummate mastery, and there is not the slightest evidence to show that he could have excelled in any other art . . . He came just at the propitious moment. Fifty years earlier he would have lacked the incentive which he found in the political and spiritual ferment of the late eighteenth century. Fifty years later he would no longer have found his native dialect in its full vigour and purity. It would already have been declining to what it has now become—an accent rather than a dialect.' What home-truths one can utter when one is well away from home!

MY BONNIE DEARIE

THE DANCE GAED THRO' THE LICHTED HA'

2 · *Mainly Biographical*

THE bare facts of Robert Burns's life can be quite briefly told, since that life extended over only thirty-seven years. He was born at the village of Alloway close to the town of Ayr on the 25th January, 1759. In a long autobiographical letter he wrote to Dr. John Moore in 1787 he frankly admits the poverty of his home and his upbringing, and the unavailing fight of his father, a tenant-farmer, to overcome that poverty. But in the same letter he dwells much more upon his own 'strong appetite for sociability' by which, from his earliest days, he was able to keep 'a heart aboon misfortunes a''. This 'appetite', whatever vagaries and dubieties of conduct it was to provoke, was a sure sign of the artistic temperament innate in Burns, and it was to this, quite as much as to the very reputable schooling he had from his father as well as from various dominies, that we owe the poet that was to be.

When in the year 1773 he 'first committed the sin of rhyme', it is significant that the lyric he wrote in praise of the young girl he worked with in the harvest-field should have been set to the tune of her favourite reel. It is no less significant that in 1775 he first earned his righteous father's disapproval and 'dislike' by going against his wishes, and indeed forbiddance, to a country dancing-school where his primary intention, in his own phrase, was 'to give his manners a brush'. From his middle teens onwards it was obvious that Burns was conscious of the poet within him, and that he was not going to be content to be an ordinary plough-man and reaper like his associates. Song was already in his heart, and in the Scottish folk tunes and folk dances of the Kyle district of Ayrshire where he had his frugal and pinched upbringing, he found the raw material for the poetry that was to be his life-work. He did not neglect the hard work he was obliged to do. Indeed he undermined his health by it. His constitution, despite his stocky build, was never very strong right from the start.

In this same long letter the young poet tells us that his life-motto was from the first *'Vive l'amour et vive la bagatelle'*, and it is not difficult to imagine the shocked face of his father, William Burnes or Burness, if his son ever said the words aloud in his presence. Incidentally the poet's father, who had moved from his native Kincardineshire in the north-east to Ayrshire in the south-west where he settled in the village of Alloway on the River Doon, was a man of considerable force of character. He was also grave, high-principled, and sensitive, and he appears to have been remarkably well-read for one in his hard-working station. He had come from a part of Scotland where the people were by tradition Jacobite, Tory, and Episcopalian. William Burness chose for a wife one Agnes Broun (almost certainly pronounced *broon* in the way still prevailing in Ayrshire). She was a farmer's daughter from Craigenton, a remote farm in the parish of Kirkoswald which is in Carrick or Southern Ayrshire. Agnes Broun appears to have been comely and fair-haired but quite illiterate, in marked contrast to her tall, swarthy, and intelligent husband. Her forbears had been tenant farmers since the Battle of Bannock-burn, and it was the tradition in this family to be fanatically Whig and Presbyterian. There were seven children of this strangely mixed marriage.

In the winter of 1781 young Robert Burns temporarily gave up both poetry and farming and went to the coast-town of Irvine to learn the trade of a flax-heckler (or dresser), largely because his father had been experimenting with the growing of flax without having learned the craft of dressing the crop when gathered. The venture failed, and Burns had soon to return to the farm of his father, whom he found at death's door. Yet in his stay of seven months at Irvine several important things happened to the young poet. One is that he made the acquaintance of the poems of Robert Fergusson, an Edinburgh poet who died at the early age of twenty-four, and whose work stimulated Burns's muse in the most striking way. Another is that he made the friendship of a young sea-captain called Richard Brown, five or six years his senior. It has often been said that Brown did Burns more harm than good (see a later chapter). But we have Burns's own admission that it was Brown who gave the young poet the notion of having his verses printed. It is certain that when Burns returned to his father's farm at Lochlie, Fergusson's work had become his inspiration and his guide. It is no less certain that in his first publication—the *Kilmarnock Poems* of 1786—the direct influence of Fergusson is strikingly evident, both in the form and in the subject of the verses. The oddest thing about the *Kilmarnock Poems* is that they contain so few of the songs or singable lyrics with which Burns began his writing and in which he was later to excel. It seems that he was merely content meanwhile to model himself upon Fergusson, and to succeed in surpassing him on domestic and pastoral subjects. It should be added here—though partisan critics of Burns too seldom add it—that the celebrated 'Burns Stanza' (six lines rhyming *a,a,a,b,a,b,* with the *a* lines having four heavy stresses, and the *b* only two) was Fergusson's invention, and therefore should be much more accurately and justly known as the 'Fergusson Stanza'. Here is an example of Fergusson's own, the beginning and the ending of his poem *The Daft Days.* (It must perhaps be explained to the Southron that the festive season in Scotland, embracing Christmas or Yule, Hogmanay, the New Year, and Handsel Monday—the first Monday in the New Year—was given this appellation on account of the mad frolics that were invariably indulged in at this time of the year.

ROBERT FERGUSSON

They still are, throughout Scotland, but unhappily the term 'the Daft Days' has fallen into desuetude.)

> Now murk December's dowie face
> Glowers owre the rigs wi' sour grimace,
> While, through his *minimum* o' space,
>   The bleer-e'ed sun,
> Wi' blinkin' light and stealin' pace,
>   His race doth run.

Frae naked groves nae birdie sings;
To shepherd's pipe nae hillock rings;
The breeze nae odorous flavour brings
    Frae Borean cave;
And dwynin' Nature droops her wings,
    Wi' visage grave . . .

Let mirth abound; let social cheer
Invest the dawnin' o' the year;
Let blythesome innocence appear,
    To crown our joy;
Nor envy wi' sarcastic sneer,
    Our bliss destroy.

And thou, great god of *aqua vitae!*
Who sway'st the empire o' this city—
When fou, we're sometimes capernoity—
    Be thou prepar'd
To hedge us frae that black banditte,
    The City Guard.

I submit that it is clear even from this random fragment that Fergusson could be as good as all but the very best of Burns, and that to appreciate his quality one only has to be told that 'dowie' means 'sombre and miserable' and that 'capernoity' is expressive old Scotch for 'quarrelsome in drink'. But to our tale of the young poet who so throve and so fostered himself on Fergusson.

Burns's luck on the land, like his father's before him, was fantastically bad. The eleven hundred square miles making up Ayrshire contained many rich and fruitful acres, but there were still more stretches of bog, mossy moors, and stony soil. These for generations would defy the progressive spirit and the new farming methods which were being introduced at the very end of the eighteenth century. And the irony of it was that the land was fetching higher rents because of new methods, even where these new methods had not yet penetrated. William Burness and his sons after him strove in vain—and for the father fatally—to wrest a bare living from the sour and stony soil of a succession of farms —Mount Oliphant near Ayr, Lochlie near Tarbolton, Mossgiel near Mauchline, and finally Ellisland near Dumfries. But while he was depressingly and continuously failing as a farmer, Burns was finding himself as a poet, and of this aspect of his life at Mauchline there is an inspired description in Catherine Carswell's biography, a book which, for such passages, has never been surpassed in sheer eloquence that is built upon both insight and scholarship:

'To realize to the full how amazing was the output of this productive period we must read, as it were at a breath, all the poems belonging to it. As we do this we receive, apart from all separate impressions, that intoxicating sense of energy released, of careless power, of rejoicing certainty and laughing ease, which place him once and for all in the enviable situation of being a people's poet of full stature. Here, we say, there must have been a conscious and practised artist at work. Yet we cannot surely declare where his art begins or ends and where nature speaks untutored, using him as her astonished mouthpiece. We feel that, while nobody but Burns could have written these poems, these

ELLISLAND

poems surprised nobody more than Burns himself. In the last resort—as indeed with all true poetry, but here in a peculiar degree—we conclude that there is no accounting for them. We can only note and ponder the circumstances in which they came into being.'

Exactly the same might be said of artists in other spheres who rejoiced almost to the extent of being surprised at their own inspiration and spontaneity, and who, like Burns, died pitiably young. One thinks particularly of Mozart and of Schubert in music, and in Burns's own art of John Keats who died at twenty-five and who opined in one of his letters that if poetry comes not as naturally as the leaves to a tree, it had better not come at all.

Burns was exactly halfway through his twenty-eighth year when the first volume of his verse was published. This was the famous Kilmarnock edition with the title, *Poems Chiefly in the Scottish Dialect*. It was published by John Wilson of Kilmarnock on July 31st, 1786, and it cost three shillings per copy. The edition numbered 612 copies and it was sold out in just over a month after publication. In short Burns may be said, as Byron said of himself, to have awakened one morning to find himself famous. Burns's own preface to the volume is both honest and modest, and not perhaps so well known as it ought to be. In one passage he pays an indirect acknowledgment to the sailor-friend at Irvine, Captain Richard Brown, who first suggested the possibility of having his verses printed: 'Though a Rhymer from his earliest years, at least from the earliest impulses of the softer passions, it was not till very lately that the applause, perhaps the partiality, of friendship, wakened his vanity so far as to make any thing of his worth showing; and none of the following works were ever composed with a view to the press. To amuse himself with the little creations of his own fancy, amid the toils and fatigues of a laborious life; to transcribe the various feelings, the loves, the griefs, the hopes, the fears in his own breast; to find some kind of counterpoise to the struggles of a world, always an alien scene, a task uncouth to the poetical mind; these were his motives for courting the Muses, and in these he found Poetry to be its own reward.'

And in the other quotable passage Burns frankly and grate-fully acknowledges the strong influences of Robert Fergusson and of Allan Ramsay before him: 'To the genius of a Ramsay, or the glorious dawnings of poor unfortunate Fergusson, he, with equal unaffected sincerity, declares that, even in his highest pulse of vanity, he has not the most distant pretensions. These two justly admired Scotch Poets he has often had in his eye in the following pieces; but rather with a view to kindle at their flame, than for servile imitation.'

Reviews of the little book, in both London and Edinburgh magazines, were gracious and long, but there is a very significant paragraph in the *Edinburgh Evening Courant* of 13th November, 1787, which said of Burns two weeks before he arrived in the capital: 'The county of Ayr is perhaps superior to any in Scotland in number of Peers, Nobles and wealthy Commoners; and yet not one of them has on this occasion stepped forth as a patron to this man, nor has any attempt been made to interest the public in his favour. His poems are read, his genius applauded, and he is left to his fate.'

Only nine months later appeared the first Edinburgh edition of Burns's poems, published by William Creech, by subscription 'for the sole benefit of the author', the publication date being the 22nd April, 1787. A month before this the poet wrote an ex-planatory letter to his friend and patroness, Mrs. Dunlop: 'I have both a second and third edition going on as the second was begun with too small a number of copies. The whole I have printed is three thousand. The price to subscribers was five shillings, to other purchasers six.' As with the Kilmarnock edition, Burns assumed all personal responsibility. On 17th April—i.e. five days before publication—Burns disposed of the property of his poems to the publisher Creech in a 'Memorandum of Agreement'.

The second Edinburgh edition—the last to appear in Burns's lifetime—was also published by Creech, the date being 18th February, 1793. This was in two volumes, 'greatly enlarged with New Poems'. One of these new poems in the extra fifty pages was nothing less than *Tam o' Shanter*. This had been written appar-ently in the course of a single inspired day at the Ellisland farm.

Let us revert, though, to the first Edinburgh edition and note the circumstances connected with its appearance. Burns had been introduced to the publisher Creech by his first important patron, young Lord Glencairn, who had an intimate and enthusiastic interest in the poet and everything about him. Creech was to behave towards Burns with the oddest mixture of meanness and generosity. But the nobleman is much the more interesting character. He was some ten years older than Burns and died five years before him (in 1791). He was James Cunningham, the 14th Earl of Glencairn. He had served in his youth as a captain in the West Fencible Regiment. From 1780 to 1784 he was one of the Representative Scotch Peers in the House of Lords. His factor, Alexander Dalziel, drew the Earl's attention to the Kilmarnock edition of the poems, by which he was much impressed. When Burns arrived in Edinburgh—incidentally he arrived there on the back of a pony which he had borrowed from an Ochiltree farmer!—the young Lord Glencairn was one of the first to make him cordially welcome. He introduced him to many influential members of the Edinburgh gentry. One of these was the Dean of the Faculty of Advocates, Henry Erskine, who, in his turn, introduced the farmer-poet to the Duchess of Gordon. This last was a great but somewhat eccentric character, quick-witted and good-natured but with a 'singular coarseness of speech', a not uncommon characteristic among the Edinburgh gentry (as Chopin was to discover and note some sixty years later). She lived on until 1812, and there was an occasion when she told Sir Walter Scott that Burns was the only man of her acquaintance whose conversation carried her off her feet (whatever, exactly, that may mean). Young Lord Glencairn seems to have been no less carried off his feet in 1786. Burns was afterwards to describe the nobleman as his 'titular Protector', and he wrote of him to Mrs. Dunlop: 'The noble Earl of Glencairn, to whom I owe more than any man of earth, does me the honour of giving me his strictures; his hints with respect to impropriety or indelicacy. I follow implicitly.'

When the subscription list for the Edinburgh edition of Burns's poems was opened, Lord Glencairn and his mother took

THE EARL
OF GLENCAIRN

twenty-four copies. And it was a direct result of Glencairn's influence that within ten days of the poet's arrival in Edinburgh, the Caledonian Hunt subscribed 'universally, one and all', which accounted for one hundred copies. On 4th May, 1787, the poet, about to leave Edinburgh, sent the Earl a grateful letter thanking him for 'all that patronage, that benevolence, and that friendship with which you have honoured me'. In January, 1788, when Burns arrived at his decision to enter the Excise Service, he wrote to Glencairn to ask his assistance. But it would seem—according to the biographer, Lockhart—that Glencairn was here helpful only indirectly. Burns's actual letter is not in his noblest or most worthy style:

'I wish to get into the Excise. I am told your lordship will easily procure me the grant from the commissioners; and your lordship's patronage and kindness which have already rescued me from obscurity, wretchedness, and exile, embolden me to ask that interest. You have likewise put it in my power to save the little tie of *home*, that sheltered an aged mother, two brothers, and three sisters from destruction. [This is very near the heart-wringing language of melodrama.] There, my lord, you have bound me over to the highest gratitude. My heart sinks within me at the idea of applying to any other of The Great who have honoured me with their countenance. I am ill qualified to dog the heels of greatness with the impertinence of solicitation; and tremble nearly as much at the thought of the cold promise as of the cold denial.'—Not much evidence here of that 'proud and sturdy independence of character' which the idolaters are for ever praising in their poet!

To offset this we may repeat what Josiah Walker wrote about the impression made by Burns on Edinburgh society: 'His person, though strong and well-knit and much superior to what might be expected in a ploughman, is still rather coarse in outline. His emotions are firm and decided, though without any pretentions to grace. In conversation he is powerful. His conceptions and expression are of corresponding vigor, and on all subjects are as remote as possible from commonplaces.'

And again: 'After breakfast [at Dr. Blacklock's] I requested him to communicate some of his unpublished pieces. I paid particular attention to his recitation, which was plain, slow, articulate and forcible but without any eloquence or art. He was standing during the time with his face towards the window to which—and not to his auditors—he directed his eyes. The day after I supped in company with him at Professor Blair's. The other guests had been invited to have an opportunity of meeting with the poet-ploughman. Though he therefore furnished the greatest proportion of the conversation, he did no more than what he saw evidently was expected. Men of genius are often prone to commit blunders in company from ignorance or negligence of the laws of conversation. From singularities of this sort Burns is unusually free.'

This seems to me well observed and well expressed, conveying, as the passage does, that Burns did not read his own poetry with any affected expressiveness and that he had a natural holding in good manners in any kind of company.

Yet Josiah Walker is not beloved of the Burns-worshippers. He is an interesting character, none the less. He was the son of an Ayrshire minister, and by two years was Burns's junior. He graduated at Edinburgh and became private tutor thereafter to the young Marquis of Tullibardine. Some eight years after Burns's remarkable success in Edinburgh, Walker was to visit the poet for two days at Dumfries. This was in November, 1795, just before Burns entered the six-months decline which ended in his death. In 1811 Walker wrote a memoir of Burns as a preface to an edition of the poems. He has a narration of taking Burns to the Globe Inn at Dumfries, and of the poet 'firing off epigrams and laying down the law between intervals calling for more drink'. For this one of the most devoted of the Burns scholars has the comment: 'One may surmise that Burns's abrupt and decisive manner was due to irritation at being patronized by an ass.' But Walker was a just critic and no ass. Far from being an ass, he became Collector of Customs at Perth in 1796, and later the editor of *The Perth Courier;* finally he became Professor of Humanity (i.e. Latin) at Glasgow University in 1815, and died there in 1831. With the idolaters any man is condemned as an ass who so much as implies that Burns was ever the worse of drink. 'Twas ever thus, and 'twill ever be so. To Walker, at least, we owe some of the best and most vivid contemporary descriptions of Burns as he appeared to the Edinburgh gentry. He describes the poet's 'dark and luxuriant sensibility', and his 'luminous expression', and declares that 'he indeed is favoured in personal appearance'. In an appendix I quote in one of my Burns speeches a still more vivid and frank description by Walker of Burns as he appeared to a room full of personages anxious to meet him.

I make no apology for dwelling far more upon the views of intelligent observers like Josiah Walker than upon the details of Burns's love-life. It is no exaggeration to say that nearly all of the women he enjoyed were dumb and stupid and easy game. There is hardly a scrap of their handwriting to prove that they felt Burns's manly heart beating against their breasts. There are two exceptions to this general rule. One is Jean Armour, the buxom and fertile girl whom Burns was eventually obliged to marry, and who showed great tolerance as well as perspicacity by uttering a single remark which is one of the world's master-pieces of understatement: 'Oor Robin should hae had twa wives!' The other exception is the Edinburgh grass-widow Mrs. McLehose, whose many love-letters to the poet, signed Clarinda, are even more unspontaneous and affected than his to her, signed Sylvander. But it is at least to the credit of Clarinda that she inspired *Ae Fond Kiss,* an exquisite lyric if ever there was one.

Far more interesting, though almost unbearably sad, are the decline and catastrophe of Burns's young life. Many Scots to this day are up in arms if any non-Scot ventures to suggest that Burns died of alcoholism. Some thirty years ago a Scottish doctor, Sir James Crichton-Browne, produced a short book called *Burns From a New Point of View* which gave plentiful evidence that Burns died of endo-carditis. But Sir James, like an inexpert advocate, gave rather too much evidence against as well as for.

On 31st January of his fatal year Burns himself wrote to his friend Mrs. Dunlop: 'I have late drunk deep of the cup of affliction. The autumn robbed me of my only daughter and darling child, and that at a distance too, and so rapidly as to put it out of my power to pay the last duties to her. I had scarcely begun to recover from that shock, when I became myself the victim of a most severe rheumatic fever—and long the die spun doubtful, until after many weeks of a sick bed I am beginning to crawl across my room, and once indeed have been before my own door in the street.'

The following month he was sufficiently recovered to crawl across to the Globe Inn as well. Sir James frankly admits this: 'He went one evening to his old howff, the Globe Inn, and found some of his old friends there, and sadly must the poor man have wanted change and good cheer, after four months' seclusion in the stuffy little bedroom in the humble house in the Mill Vennel.' Here he quotes Dr. James Currie, Burns's first biographer: 'He dined at a tavern and returned home at three in the

PORTRAIT BY ALEXANDER NASMYTH

morning, benumbed and intoxicated. This was followed by an attack of rheumatism which confined him to bed for a week.' This Sir James dismisses, in spite of printing it, as 'a wholly inaccurate narration', and then goes on making matters worse still: 'The more detailed account of this incident, preserved by tradition in Dumfries, and everywhere accepted as authentic, is that on leaving a jovial party in the Globe Inn he was, on reaching the door, overpowered by the effects of the liquor he had drunk, fell to the ground, which was covered with snow, and lay there asleep for some hours. Under these circumstances, being reduced by the action of strong medicine prescribed by Dr. Maxwell, a fatal chill penetrated his bones, and fostered the seeds of rheumatism already in possession of his debilitated body. The whole thing is perhaps a myth, but if he fell down on leaving the Globe Inn, the probability is, not that he was over-powered by the drink he had taken, but that he fainted from heart failure. From a sudden syncope he would recover in a little, but alcoholic coma on a bed of snow must have ended in death. Mrs. Burns, the best and most straightforward of witnesses, testified, as we have seen, that he never came home in an incapable state; and in recalling the details of his last illness, she is not likely to have forgotten so striking a circum-stance as his midnight arrival in a half-frozen state after a fall.'

This is given for what it is worth. But I cannot pretend that it is cogently argued, and, *pace* Mrs. Burns, it might easily have been that, on this occasion at least, the poor dear man did not come home in an incapable state, for the simple reason that he was incapable of coming home at all.

In February Burns had a relapse and a severe repercussion of rheumatic fever; and thereafter his life slowly ebbed away for the five months remaining to him. His own words near the end make piteous reading: 'In these eight or nine months I have been ailing, sometimes bed-fast, sometimes not. For the last three months I have been tortured with an excruciating rheumatism which has reduced me to nearly the last stage. Pale, emaciated, so feeble as occasionally to need help from my chair, my spirits fled! fled!'

Yet even in April and May and June he was writing to George Thomson and James Johnson on the subject of their collections of old Scottish songs and airs. To Thomson he writes describing his pains, but can conclude on a distinctly gayer note: 'This will be delivered to you [at Edinburgh] by a Mrs. Hyslop, landlady of the Globe Tavern here, which for these many years has been my Howff, and where our friend Clarke and I have had many a merry squeeze . . .'

In May he writes a business letter to Thomson concluding: 'I have great hopes that the genial influence of the approaching summer will set me to rights, but as yet I cannot boast of returning health. I have no reason to believe that my complaint is a flying gout—a damnable business!'

Around the 1st of June he writes to Johnson: 'Personal and domestic afflictions have almost entirely banished that alacrity and life with which I used to woo the rural Muse of Scotia.' On the 26th June he writes to James Clarke (a schoolmaster friend who had borrowed money from him): 'As to my individual self, I am tranquil—I would despise myself if I were not. But Burns's poor widow, and half a dozen of his dear little ones, helpless orphans—there I am weak as a woman's tear.'

His criminal idiot of a doctor, one Maxwell, now suggested he should go to a lonely spa, Brow Well on the Solway, and try sea-bathing and horse-riding as a cure for his condition. Whatever his misgiving may have been about this desperate remedy, he went to Brow Well alone on 4th July. On that day he said to his wife that he thought he was dying, adding in a prophetic flash: 'Don't be afraid—I'll be more respected a hundred years after I am dead than I am at present.' When he reached the desolate spa his old friend Mrs. Riddell (who was on a visit in the neighbourhood) thoughtfully sent him her carriage for his use. She visited him too, and gave a subsequent vivid account: 'He seemed already touching the brink of eternity. He spoke of his death without any of the ostentation of philosophy, but with firmness as well as feeling, as an event likely to happen very soon, and which gave him concern chiefly from leaving his four children so young and unprotected, and his wife in so interesting a situation, in hourly expectation of lying-in . . . I have seldom seen his mind greater or more collected. There was frequently a considerable degree of vivacity in his sallies. We parted about sunset. The next day, 6th July, I saw him again, and we parted to meet no more.' (At one phase of my reading I added the number of the poet's *traceable* children, alive and dead, legitimate and illegitimate, and it came to sixteen.)

Crichton-Browne must have the penultimate word: 'His cure at the Brow Well, in so far as its other elements were concerned, and especially as regards the sea-bathing, in which he valiantly persevered, persuading himself that he was being strengthened thereby, cannot but have been hurtful to him. The marvel is that he survived to return to his home at Dumfries. This he did on the evening of Monday, 18th July, when his poor wife was so struck by the change in his appearance that she became speechless. From this period he was closely confined to his bed, and was scarcely himself for half-an-hour at a time.' The surgeon goes on to put up a big clinical argument that it was endo-carditis and not alcohol that killed Burns. It does not in the least alter my own conviction that he died of a complexus of ailments and weaknesses—endo-carditis certainly, but that condition had been provoked by his own physical excesses since his earliest manhood.

Burns's very last note was sent to James Armour, his father-in-law, at Mauchline, and it runs: 'Dumfries, 18th July, 1796. My dear Sir, Do, for Heaven's sake, send Mrs. Armour here immediately. My wife is hourly expecting to be put to bed. Good God! what a situation for her to be in, poor girl, without a friend! I returned from sea-bathing quarters to-day, and my medical friends would almost persuade me that I am better; but I think and feel that my strength is so gone that the disorder will prove fatal to me. Your Son-in-law. R.B.'

Three days later, on 25th July, 1796, the great poet and great lover was buried at Dumfries with full military and masonic honours. At the very moment when his body was lowered into its grave his wife, Jean Armour, was giving birth to yet another boy who was christened Alexander Cunningham Burns.

And just three days before his death the father had written a lyric and handed it to the young girl who had been nursing him. It is one of his perfect songs, and Mendelssohn was later to wed it to a melody as sweet and melancholy as the lyric itself:

> O, wert thou in the cauld blast,
>   On yonder lea, on yonder lea,
> My plaidie to the angry airt,
>   I'd shelter thee, I'd shelter thee.
> Or did Misfortune's bitter storms
>   Around thee blaw, around thee blaw,
> Thy bield should be my bosom,
>   To share it a', to share it a'.
>
> O were I in the wildest waste,
>   Sae black and bare, sae black and bare,
> The desert were a Paradise,
>   If thou wert there, if thou wert there.
> Or were I monarch of the globe,
>   Wi' thee to reign, wi' thee to reign,
> The brightest jewel in my crown
>   Wad be my queen, wad be my queen.

There is genius in those repetitions in every other line. And if Priapus was the god of Robert Burns, it is no less certain that Erato, the particular muse of the love-lyric, was his goddess.

WITHIN A MILE O' EDINBORO' TOON

WHEN HAILSTANES DRIVE WI' BITTER SKYTE

3 · His County in his Time

AYRSHIRE in Burns's time had nothing like the lush appearance it has today. The Reverend John Mitchell thus described it as it appeared some twenty years before the poet was born:

'The face of the country was far from being cultivated or inviting. On the contrary, it appeared rough and dark, consisting greatly of heath, moss, patches of straggling wood and rudely cultivated grounds. The roads, made entirely by statute labour, were not smooth but irregular in their line and far from being level in their track. The ditches which bounded them were seldom cleared out, and the hedges with which they were skirted being allowed to shoot forth in all their wild luxuriance were seldom cut and never pruned or clipped. Young trees were rarely planted, except perhaps in the hedgerow; in short, the work of rural improvement had not yet begun, and the country presented upon the whole a bleak and somewhat repulsive appearance.'

Another chronicler, Colonel William Fullerton, has these vivid passages in a Board of Agriculture Report he wrote in 1793, three years before Burns's death:

'A stranger, passing through these districts, must be surprised to observe such a multitude of agricultural defects still existing. But his applause could undeniably be excited, when he understood the great difference between the present management and that which took place forty years ago.—At that period there was hardly a practicable road in the country . . . The farm-houses were mere hovels, moated with clay, having an open hearth or fireplace in the middle, the dunghill at the door; the cattle starving, and the people wretched. The few ditches which existed were ill constructed, and the hedges worse preserved . . . no fallows—no green crops—no sown grass—no carts or waggons—no straw yards; hardly a potato, or any other esculent root, and, indeed, no garden vegetables; unless a few Scotch kail, which, with milk and oatmeal, formed the diet of the people. There was little straw, and no hay except a scanty portion of the coarsest quality collected from the bogs . . . The ground was scourged with a succession of oats after oats, as long as they would pay for seed and labour, and afford a small surplus of oatmeal for the family, and then remained in a state of absolute sterility, or over-run with thistles, till rest again persuaded it again to reproduce a scanty crop . . .'

As the winter seasons in Ayrshire were almost invariably wet as well as cold, the plough was never yoked till Candlemas. It does not appear that the farmers used more than two horses to each plough; but there was one man to hold, another to drive, a third to keep clear the mould board and to keep the coulter in the ground. The plough was, of course, of the Scotch kind; and, as the soil was almost always stiff and full of stones, it was constructed with the strongest possible materials. The cold and rainy spring made sowing late, so that oats were seldom harrowed in before April. And it was not infrequently the end of May before barley was put in the ground.

As there were few or no enclosures, the horses and cattle were either tethered during the summer months, or entrusted to the care of a herd and his dog by whom the poor animals were kept constantly on the move. They were often impelled by famine to depredate the adjacent crops. We read, too, that every farmer sowed a sufficiency of flax for the women of his family to spin in their leisure hours. A small portion of hemp was likewise planted to make sacking and other coarse materials needed on the farm. And a quantity of wool was either bought or grown for the purpose of spinning woollen stuffs to clothe the family. These as well as the linen thread were usually worked by some local weaver and thus supplied clothing for both sexes. Stalks of hemp often took the place of candles for lighting purposes, and even near the coal-fields and collieries whole months were spent in cutting, drying, and stacking peat to serve as fuel. To this day in remote farms and shepherds' crofts and cottages in Ayrshire peat is the principal fuel.

Colonel Fullerton in his Agricultural Report for 1793 (when Burns was a toddler) has this passage:

'About forty years ago, the late Earl of Eglinton, who possessed a very large and valuable property, dispersed over a great extent in the most improvable parts of Ayrshire, resolved to rescue his estates from the condition in which he found them. An eminent farmer, Mr. Wright of Ormiston, was brought from East Lothian to introduce the proper mode of ploughing, levelling ridges, farrowing, drilling, turnip-husbandry, and rotations of crops. Great attention was bestowed on the breed of horses and cattle. Ploughmen and dairy people were brought from various parts of England. Fences were made on an extensive scale, and the country was beautified by a multitude of tree-clumps, belts, and plantations. The noblemen and gentlemen very zealously concurred in promoting measures so conducive to their own advantage and to the general interest of their country. The demand for cheese and butter to supply the multiplying wants of Glasgow, Paisley, Greenock and Port-Glasgow, led to increasing care respecting milch-cows and dairies. The English market afforded ready sale for black cattle; and the growing manufactures of the country introduced the benefits of opulence.'

JOHN GALT

The Ayrshire novelist, John Galt, writing of the late eighteenth century in his still readable *Annals of the Parish*, gives us a racy taste of the life of those days in such a town as Irvine:

'It was in this year that the great smuggling trade corrupted all the west coast, especially the laigh [or low-lying] lands about the Troon and the Loans. The tea was going like the chaff, the brandy like well-water, and the wastrie of all things was terrible. There was nothing minded but the riding of cadgers by day, and excisemen by night—and battles between the smugglers and the king's men, both by sea and land. There was a continual drunkenness and debauchery; and our session, that was but on the lip of this whirlpool of antiquity, had an awful time o't. I did all that was in my power of nature to keep my people from the contagion. I preached sixteen times from the text, "Render to Caesar the things that are Caesar's". I visited, and I exhorted; I warned, and I prophesied; I told them that although the money came in like slate stones, it would go like the snow off the dyke. But for all I could do, the evil got in among us, and we had no less than three contested bastard bairns upon our hands at one time, which was a thing never heard of in a parish of the shire of Ayr since the Reformation.'

It was a thing to be infinitely more heard of in Robert Burns's heyday!

These old documents and chronicles tell us much more about the poor standard of living and of the mean dwellings of the herds or 'cote-men' and even of the farmers in those days. In certain remote steadings they are not so very much improved even today. I have in my time visited out-of-the-way Ayrshire farm-houses and cottages which have a mere but-and-ben—that is, a living-room with a big bed in it and a sitting-room which is hardly ever used except when there is a wedding or a funeral in the family.

But in matters of food and clothing, conditions in the present century are, of course, much improved. Another agricultural reporter, William Aiton, tells us, when surveying the year 1811, only fifteen years after Burns's death:

'The food and mode of living of farmers of that rank, and of the servants of farmers of all ranks, in the county of Ayr, is, for *breakfast,* abundance of good pottage made with whey, during eight or nine months, and with water during the rest of the year, always taken with plenty of milk; and either cheese or herrings with oatmeal-cakes, or milk with cakes, or frequently both cheese and milk with bread after the pottage. For *dinner,* they are allowed at least three or four times every week good substantial broth—made thick with barley, pease, beans, and garden-stuffs, with abundance of beef or mutton boiled in the broth, and eaten after them with potatoes or bread; and after the meat, as much oatcakes and milk as they are able to eat. Parts of the broth are reserved for next day, and if there is no cold beef or mutton

everyone is allowed as much cheese or fish as they can eat . . . Sometimes, instead of broth, potatoes are stewed with beef or mutton, and at other times the potatoes, being divested of their skins before they are boiled, are beaten into paste, mixed with a small quantity of good salt butter and as much sweet milk as renders them palatable. These, in the language of the district, are termed "champit potatoes" [they still are to this day in rural Ayrshire] . . .
The *supper* of small tenants, and their children and servants, as well as the servants of the more opulent and respectable tenants, is, nine times out of every ten, composed of either pottage and milk; sowens and milk [a rough form of porridge or groats]; or potatoes beaten with butter and milk as has been mentioned.'

But in Burns's own day beef and mutton were very much scarcer, and the fare was therefore more sparse and frugal. Writing in 1793, Colonel Fullerton says:

'Very little butcher-meat was used, excepting a proportion which every family salted at Martinmas, to serve during the winter with their groats, or prepared barley, and kail or broth. . . . So small was the consumption of butcher-meat in this province that there were not more than fifty head of cattle annually killed in the county town of Ayr, at this period, although it contained from 4 to 5 thousand inhabitants.'

But he is, of course, writing of a still earlier time.

William Aiton is lively again about the Ayrshire fairs which occurred in every town or village several times a year—in Mauchline as often as eleven times:

'The manner in which the unmarried people, of both sexes, conduct themselves at fairs and races, is far from being decorous, and calls loudly for reformation. Great numbers of *lads* and *lassies* are collected at the fair, in the course of the afternoon, where they continue till about midnight. The country girls travel to the fair (unless in time of frost) without shoes or stockings, with their coats tucked up, and retire to some corner of the park near the fair to put on their shoes and perform the labours of the *toilette;* after which they stalk into the fair, make *sham* calls at shops, or saunter among the crowd till their rustic admirers who are also on the *look-out*, invite them to the change-house. This is done by tapping the fair one on the shoulder, treading on her foot, or by some pantomimic gesture which she understands and readily obeys—unless a swain more to her mind shall then make other signals.

Nothing is so galling to the *lassies* as to be allowed to stand long idle in the market-place, without being invited to the change-house by some young men. The place where groups of them stand, without being called upon, is termed "the pitiful market". A "sturdy fellow" having made his signals, struts off to the ale-house, his "clever hizzy" following at a short distance, proud of having gotten a "chance", and envied by such as have had none.

In the ale-house the *lad* treats his *lass* with ale, whisky, and sweet-meats (called *fairings*), hugs her in his arms, tumbles her into a bed if one can be found (though many persons be in the room). Then, with one arm under her head, the other and one of his legs over her, he enjoys a tête-à-tête conversation, longer or shorter as the market happens to be brisk or slow. After a little time, they adjourn to some long-room, mason lodge, or barn, to dance reels.'

And William Aiton concludes:

'This is what they call "holding the fair", and it is continued till about midnight, when the *lads* and *lassies* begin to pair off, and return to the fair one's home, where they generally spend an hour or two by themselves, in the barn, byre, or cart shed, *talking over the events of the day.'*
These last italics are mine!

Aiton is no less interesting and relevant on the old customs still prevalent. Writing in the year 1811, he has this:

'Nine-tenths of the marriages of people of the lower rank in Ayrshire are still celebrated on a Friday, the day of the Scandinavian goddess, Frea. Beltane, one of the great festivals of the pagans, is still observed as a rent-term in Ayrshire; it is the day when tenants take possession of and remove from their farms. The direction in which the wind blows on Beltane morning is looked to as ominous. It is upon the morning of Beltane that those who were conversant in occult sciences were understood to run over their neighbours' fields, trailing a hair-tether after them, and thereby acquiring a power of milking from that tether the greatest part of the milk of the cows grazing in these fields throughout the summer. The practice of kindling fires on heights at Beltane is still common in the county of Ayr.' [The custom was revived, in my own recollection, on the occasion of the coronation of King George V in 1911—precisely one hundred years after Aiton's report.] Aiton continues:

'A fair at Ochiltree is kept in May, and near to Beltane the herds used to collect whins, brooms, coal, etc., and kindle fires after dark, which were attended by great numbers of the inhabitants. The same practice still obtains over other parts of the county . . . Hallowe'en, the other great festival of the pagans, is still observed, in Ayrshire, as an interesting period, and many spells are then used to discover matters of futurity—particularly respecting marriages. Many of the lower orders in that county still believe that the Devil is ready at their call on that night, and—on their using certain capers and spells—to discover a secret, which generally occupies much of their thought; namely, who is to be their future spouse . . . The manner in which these spells are conducted, and their absurdity, are properly exposed, in the poem of *Hallowe'en* by the celebrated Robert Burns.'

The difference between then and now is made abundantly clear from reading such old records. It is not that the clothes and customs differ so much—these differ not much more, and not much less, than the language as it is spoken. But the appearance of the land was utterly unrecognisable. Today if we look at the lush Ayrshire landscape we see fields that are usually square or rectangular, regular plantations of trees, neat hedges of hawthorn or beech, tidy farmsteads whitewashed or pinkwashed, and

well-made country roads. But all this lushness and polish is a
result of more than a hundred years of improvement and maintenance. More than four generations of draining and manuring
and liming and systematic cultivation have given the countryside a far brighter and smarter appearance than it had in Burns's
lifetime. The poet was particularly unlucky—as was his father—
in his choice of farms. But the whole county was not a rich one
in matter of soil before agricultural improvements were made,
and to this day a large percentage of the land is either moorland
or rough untended pasture cropped only by sheep.

There are some things, of course, that have not changed—
notably the weather. The old joke so often applied to the weather
in the Highlands applies no less to this lowland county. If you can
see Ailsa Craig from the Ayrshire coast it means it's going to rain,
and if you can't see it, it's raining already! The skies are often,
too often, obscured with the clouds that bring sudden showers
or prolonged rainfall. The sandy shores are as they always were,
and of course the hills are eternal, and so are the mountain
streams or burns that run down from the lonely hills as tribu-
taries to Ayrshire's rivers—the Irvine, the Ayr, the Doon, the
Girvan, the Stinchar, all of which pour into the Firth of Clyde.
The hills and the waters are, in short, much as they were in
Burns's time. But the plains and the farmlands and the commons
were very much shaggier and more uncouth. One old writer
tells us that 'the whole countryside had the appearance of a wild
and dreary common'. Another that much of the county was 'a
naked waste, scarce a tree appearing to gratify the wandering
eye'. In short, the Ayrshire the poet was born into was, as it had
been for centuries before, a black and poverty-stricken land with
mosses and heaths covering not only the uplands but the plains
as well. Although the countryside in the eighteenth century was
not devoid of trees—as Dr. Johnson declared the whole country
to be—nearly all of the present-day forest and woodland had
still to be planted. As I have already pointed out, the sustenance
of peasants in the country and of artisans in the town was both
frugal and monotonous. Oatmeal was taken three times a day
in one farm or another. Meat was scarce and expensive, and

many things now regarded as necessities—like sugar, tea, and even bread—were unknown to people as poorly off as Burns was. Potatoes were grown, but it was not till long after Burns's death that there was evolved the delicious early Ayrshire potato now cultivated in the sandy soil of the county, sometimes in the sand on the very seashore. It was during Burns's lifetime that a new kind of scientific farming was invented and developed. Before that the appearance of the land had probably not altered materially throughout centuries. The change which came in the course of a few years was in the nature of a complete transformation.

The world, in other aspects besides agriculture, was rapidly changing and improving even within Burns's short lifetime.

'Bliss was it in that dawn to be alive,
But to be young was very heaven'

wrote Wordsworth many years later, looking back upon his own youth. New ideas were in the air. New fields of knowledge were being developed and explored. From the French came the call for Liberty, Equality, and Fraternity with an amount of cruelty, bloodshed, and corruption, almost defeating their own declared purpose. In America a huge new independent nation was establishing itself. Even in the out of the way corners of Scotland there was happening a bloodless revolution in the Kirk. The Calvinistic and harsh dictatorship of the Kirk Session was at last being smashed, not before time, by the Seceding Movement, by the good sense and tolerance of the new Moderation ministers, and by the pungent anti-Kirk and anti-hypocrisy satires of Burns himself. Moreover, while the countryside and country landscape were being transformed by the new agricultural methods, so villages and towns were being radically altered and re-vitalised by the new industrial methods and machinery. Domestic weaving and spinning were rapidly vanishing before the developments of manufacture in specially built factories. The Industrial Revolution in Scotland was imminent at the turn of the century.

O WAD SOME POW'R THE GIFTIE GIE US
TO SEE OURSELS AS OTHERS SEE US

4·Other Times, Manners, People

THE totally different ambience of Burns's lifetime as distinct from ours may best be communicated by some extracts from the Scottish newspapers around the year of his birth. For example, I cull this from an Edinburgh evening newspaper a fortnight before the poet was born at Alloway:

> There is gone missing from his father's house in the parish of St. Lawrence, a YOUNG LAD, aged 20 years, with red bushy hair, wearing a small blue bonnet, snuff coloured cloaths, black kilt breeches, white plaiden hose, his speech scarcely to be understood, quite simple in his behaviour. Any person who can give any notice of him, 'tis begged they would keep, entertain him, and send word thereof to the publisher of this paper, they shall be handsomely rewarded for their trouble and expence. *Edinburgh Evening Courant*—January 11th, 1759

And this is a bucolic advertisement unimaginable today:

ADVERTISEMENT: TO LEAP THIS SEASON
At Mr. Robert Swan's in March-hall nigh Edinburgh, at a

guinea and a half each mare, and half a crown to the keeper, the famous high-bred horse, YOUNG SNIP, a beautiful bay, seven years old, fifteen hands high, free from all natural blemishes, and is allowed by all judges to be as beautiful a stallion as any in England. He was bred by Sir William Middleton in Belsay-castle . . .

N.B. Good grass for mares and proper care.—The money to be paid at the stable door, or when the mares are taken away. —The horse will be down from England about the middle of April. *Edinburgh Evening Courant*—March 27th, 1759

And this notice, bright as an old engraving:

THE LONDON STAGE COACH
continues to set out every other Tuesday, from John Somerville's in the Canongate, Edinburgh, and from Hosea Eastgate's, removed from the Coach and Horses in Dean Street, Soho, to the Crown Yard in Silver Street, Golden Square, London; where places may be taken for said Coach: Likewise waiting Jobs, or Coaches and Horses to be had in any Part of England. By your humble Servant. HOSEA EASTGATE
The Caledonian Mercury—February, 1759

And this, indicating the therapeutics of the times:

ADVT. By the KING'S ROYAL LETTERS PATENT
DR. BATEMAN'S PECTORAL DROPS
One Shilling the Bottle, which is three DOSES (and operates only by moderate Sweat and Urine, after which keep warm). Which, for more than 24 Years, are universally known to be the safest and surest Relief in the most acute RHEUMATISM, Pains in the Breast, Limbs and Joints, slow and latent FEVERS (preferable to any Powders) a single Dose remarkably stops the Progress of a Cold, and certainly prevents the ill Consequences arising from that very common Disorder, the Forerunner of almost all Distempers . . .
Dr. Fraunce's Female Strengthening Elixir, 1s. 6d. the Bottle.
Dr. Hooper's Female Pills, 40 in a Box for 1s.

Baron Schwanberg's Liquid Shell, being a safe and sure Dissolvent of the Stone and Gravel, gives immediate relief in the Strangury, Wind-cholick, Disorders in the Stomach and Bowels of Infants, preferable to any cordial, 1s. 6d. the Bottle.

The true Daffey's Elixir, at 1s. 3d. per Bottle.

Betton's true genuine British Oil, for Wounds, Bruises, Ulcers, &c, 1s. 6d.

Dr. Bateman's golden and plain Spirits of Scurvy Grass, 1s.

Dr. Stoughton's great Stomachic Elixir, 1s.

Chase's Balsamick Pills for the Asthmas, &c, 2s.

Dr. Anderson's, or the true Scots Pills, 1s. the Bot.

The Seaman's Balsam, 1s. 6d.

True Eau de Luce, 3s. the large and 1s. 6d. the small Bottle.

Right Hungary, and fine double-distilled Lavender Waters, &c.

Observe that the names DICEY and OKELL be in all the Direction Bills. *The Caledonian Mercury*—March, 1759

And this occasional verse from *The Caledonian Mercury* for April 24th of the same year:

On George Frederick Handel, Esq. who performed the Messiah on the 6th, and died the 14th inst.

To melt the Soul, to captivate the Ear,
Angels his Melody might deign to hear.
T'anticipate on Earth the Joys of Heaven
Was Handel's Task; to him the Power was given!
Ah! when he late attun'd Messiah's Praise;
With Sounds celestial, with melodious Lays;
A last Farewell his languid Looks express'd,
And thus, methinks, th'enraptur'd Crowd address'd:
'Adieu, my dearest Friends! and also you,
Joint Sons of sacred Harmony, adieu!
A whisp'ring Angel prompts me to retire,
Bids me prepare to meet th'immortal Choir!
O for the glorious Change,' great Handel cry'd;
Messiah heard his Voice—and Handel dy'd.

And this advertisement in the same paper in the same year
(May 26th):

This Day is published
And sold at the Shop of W. Millar
THE HISTORY OF RASSELAS
PRINCE OF ABISSINIA. A tale
By the Author of the Rambler
In Two Volumes
London: Printed for R. and J. Dodsley, Pall-mall
and W. Johnstone, Ludgate-street.

And this public notice which gives the period's atmosphere:

All gentlemen volunteers that are willing and able to serve his
Majesty King George (II), in the corps of light cavalry
ordered to be raised under the command of the Right
Honourable the Lord Aberdour, let them apply to Lieutenant
Maitland in Haddingtown; or at Lord Selkirk's house at
St. Mary Isle near Kirkcudbright; Colonel Haliburton's, at
Haliburton near Coupar in Angus; Captain Buchanan's at
Drumpellier, near Glasgow; Mr. Robert Gardiner's office in
the Canongate, or Thomas Wood's Inn-keeper at Kelso.

They shall enter into present pay; receive two guineas
bounty, and a crown to drink his majesty's health; have
compleat new clothing, arms and accoutrements, be well
mounted on able active horses, and have everything necessary
for the equipment of a compleat cavalier.

Proper encouragement will be given to those who bring
volunteers that shall be approved of.

GOD SAVE THE KING

N.B. Over and above the County given by his lordship, all
volunteers engaging in this corps will receive a share of the
gratuity offered by the Gentlemen of the Signet very gener-
ously, to promote the completing his majesty's corps recruiting
at Edinburgh. *Edinburgh Evening Courant* —December 6th, 1759

And this, from the same paper, which gives the tone of the times even more vividly:

LETTER TO THE EDITOR: SIR, At this time, when we are threatened with an invasion, and are told that M. Thurot's squadron is actually sailed for that purpose, I presume the following piece will be acceptable to the publick. It is the instructions which that most excellent officer, the late Major-General Wolfe thought proper to give to the 20th regiment of foot (of which he was then Lieut. Col.) while they were quartered at Canterbury, in the latter end of the year, 1755), on a like supposition of a descent on our coast.

The thoughts of so great a man must be respectable to every one; and certainly these may be of great use to all our regiments, in case anything of the like nature should happen. Indeed it is much to be wished that, in general, only such sensible and useful things, as these destructions direct were practised by our troops, instead of trifles calculated for shew. It should however be observed, that as these instructions relate only to the battle he then commanded, they ought not to be taken in a more extensive view, but as calculated merely to instruct the men and officers of that corps. And to instil into them that valour, prudence and judgment, which he himself possessed in so excellent a degree. But, to enlarge any further upon this piece, would be doing injustice to the abilities of its author. I shall therefore only beg to join with the universal voice of the public in lamenting the loss of the best officer, and man of the greatest genius in our service, and I might almost say, in our century.

I am, Sir, Your very humble servant, A.B.

A news paragraph in the same issue begins:

The universal consternation the surrender of Quebeck has occasioned in France cannot easily be expressed.

Again, from a weekly London paper in the year of Burns's birth. It is *The Monitor* or *British Freeholder*:

A brief account of the memorable year 1758, in which we

have seen the British flag restored to its ancient dignity, and our enemies obliged to yield up the dominion of the seas, to the superiority of the British navy.

A year, which will for ever record the wisdom of our national councils; the conduct of our officers, and the bravery of our men employed in the public service, both by sea and land; and the cheerfulness with which all ranks of people contributed to their support . . . What has exalted Britain to its present power and glory? Its naval strength duly employed. What has humbled France? The British power by sea, levelled against her shipping, her coasts, all her settlements. What has made this nation respectable to the rest of Europe? Her formidable fleets and wise ministry . . .

We may read this a shade ruefully today!

And, also in London, from the *Gentleman's Magazine* for July, 1787. This issue printed among its select poetry the Burns poem, 'On a Scotch Bard, Gone to the West Indies' (beginning 'A' ye wha live by sowps o' drink') as being 'from the poems of Robert Burns, an Ayrshire Ploughman' and recommends the reader to a book-review in the same issue:

'I know not if I shall be accused of enthusiasm and partiality when I introduce to the notice of my readers a poet of our own country, with whose writings I have lately become acquainted; but, if I am not greatly deceived, I think I may safely pronounce him a genius of no ordinary rank. The person to whom I allude is Robert Burns, an Ayrshire ploughman, whose poems were some time ago published in a country town in the West of Scotland, with no other ambition, it would seem, than to circulate among the inhabitants of the county where he was born, to obtain a little fame from those who had heard of his talents. I hope I shall not be thought to assume too much, if I endeavour to place him in a higher point of view, to call for a verdict of his country on the merit of his works, and to claim for him those honours which their excellence appears to deserve.

'In mentioning the circumstances of his humble station, I

mean not to rest his pretensions solely on that title, or to weigh
the merits of his poetry when considered in relation to the
lowness of his birth, and the little opportunity of improvement
which his education could afford. These particulars, indeed,
might excite our wonder at his productions; but his poetry, considered abstractly, and without the apologies arising from his
situation, seems to me fully entitled to command our feelings,
and to obtain our applause. *One bar, indeed, his birth and education
have opposed to his fame, the language in which most of his poems are
written. Even in Scotland, the provincial dialect which Ramsay and he
have used, is now read with a difficulty which greatly damps the pleasure
of the reader; in England it cannot be read at all, without such a constant
reference to a Glossary as nearly to destroy their pleasure.* [Italics mine!]

'Some of his productions, however, especially those of the grave
style, are almost English. From one of these I shall first present
my readers with an extract . . . from THE VISION, in which the
Genius of his native county, Ayrshire, is supposed to address
him . . .'

The reviewer quotes six stanzas, then commends the 'rapt and
inspired melancholy' of the poem, and goes on to praise the same
quality in *Despondency, Winter: A Dirge, Invocation to Ruin*: 'Of the
tender and the moral, specimens equally advantageous might be
drawn from such elegiac verses as *Man was Made to Mourn* and
from *The Cotter's Saturday Night*'. He proceeds to quote the whole
of *To A Mouse* 'not from its superior merit, but because its length
suits the bounds of my paper'.

Thereafter he observes:

'I have seldom met with an image more truly pastoral than
that of the lark, in the second stanza. Such strokes as these mark
the pencil of the poet, which delineates nature with the precision
of intimacy, yet with the delicate colouring of beauty and of
taste.'

He continues a little later:

'I am very far from meaning to compare our rustic bard to
Shakespeare, yet whoever will read his lighter and more
humorous poems . . . will perceive with what uncommon
punctuation and sagacity this heaven-taught ploughman, from

his humble and unlettered station, has looked upon men and manners.'

It is to be regretted that Burns met so few of his host of brilliant contemporaries. Among the poets who were living at exactly the same time were Goethe and Schiller in Germany, André Chénier in France, in Italy the proud and noble Alfieri, and in England a constellation including William Blake (born two years before Burns), the boy-poet Thomas Chatterton, and William Cowper. Coleridge was born in 1772 when Burns was thirteen, and Byron, Keats and Shelley first came into existence only a year or two before Burns's death.

In 1795, the year before Burns's death, the inimitable biographer and diarist, James Boswell, breathed his last at the age of fifty-four. He could and ought to have met the poet, and never did. Some years ago I set a competition in a London literary weekly for a conversation between two literary contemporaries who never met in reality. Competitors were asked to imagine the inter-reaction at a meeting between Boswell and Burns, or any other such pair of contemporaries who never did meet. One entrant made Boswell write in his journal about Burns: 'His verse is unlikely to have that universal appeal he seeks.' And another and better one had him write when he was on a visit to his father in Ayrshire: 'I was waited on this morning by Mr. Burns. He is a farmer near Auchlinleck, a curious, odd fellow, who has printed some stanzas.'

But these, of course, are mere ebullitions of fancy. The pity of it is that the two might easily have come face to face and struck fire from one another's flint. Auchinleck is in the same part of Ayrshire as Mauchline, and indeed a bare five miles distant. But in the year 1784, when Burns moved to the farm of Mossgiel near Mauchline, Boswell was in London recording the last days of the life of Dr. Johnson. And in 1787, when Burns was in Edinburgh enjoying his triumph, Boswell was in London hard at work on his great biography. It is odd and disappointing that there is no mention whatever of Burns in that biography, no direct allusion in the journals that have so far appeared, and none whatever in Boswell's published letters which range between 1758 (the year before Burns's birth) and 1795 (the year before his death). Boswell himself died in 1795, on the 19th May.

Another misfortune is that Burns never met and therefore never had his portrait done by Sir Henry Raeburn, Scotland's greatest portrait-painter. Raeburn was born in Edinburgh in 1756, but at the time of Burns's visit he was just finishing his studies in Rome. He was later to paint many great Scots including Hume, Scott, and Boswell himself. We therefore have to be content with the all-too-familiar and rather shallow portrait by Alexander Nasmyth. Better, at once more satisfying and deeper, is the chalk drawing by Archibald Skirving, which is said to be 'based' on the Nasmyth. Scott himself declared this to be the only true likeness of the poet. But in spite of the drawing's excellence and conviction, there is evidence that Skirving like Raeburn was in Italy when Burns was in Edinburgh and never actually set eyes on him. The original drawing was the property of George Thomson, the collector of Scottish songs for whom Burns did much research.

Burns's sole meeting with Walter Scott, then only a boy of fifteen, is described in Scott's own words in another chapter. Alas, that he did not come face to face with any other of the truly distinguished men and women of his age, and that he came no farther south than Carlisle and Newcastle. Yet his life coincided with that of Sheridan and Burke and Fox and Horace Walpole in London. It coincided, too, with that of his formidable rival as an amorist, Casanova; with that of the social reformer, Robert Owen; and with that of the matchless Mozart who was born in 1756 and who died, like Burns, when he was well under forty.

In Burns's last few years of life the French Revolution reached its furious height, and he lived till July, 1796, to see its fury spent. Both King Louis XVI and his queen, Marie-Antoinette, were guillotined in the year 1793. Within the same twelvemonth Marat was stabbed to death in his bath, and many other leading revolutionaries, including Robespierre and Danton and Fouquier-Tinville, were all guillotined. These executions were dignified compared with what happened to the Princesse de

DRAWING BY ARCHIBALD SKIRVING

Lamballe in September, 1792. She had refused to take the oath expressing detestation of the monarchy, and when she left the court-room she was cut to the ground, her severed head was paraded on a pike in front of the Queen's windows; and finally her heart was roasted and eaten. It may have been the age of enlightenment. But it contained bloodshed enough to be the age of savagery as well.

THE AULD CLAY BIGGIN

5 · Mainly Chronological

1759, JANUARY 25th. Robert Burns born at Alloway near Ayr in the Kyle section of Ayrshire. He was the eldest son of William Burnes (who so spelled the name) and whose dates were 1721–1784. Burns's mother was Agnes Broun (pronounced *broon*) whose dates were 1732–1820. It is not generally realised that Mrs. Burns or Burnes survived her famous son by nearly twenty-four years. The other children were Gilbert (1760–1827), Agnes (1762–1834), Anabelle (1764–1832), William (1767–1790), and Isabella (1771–1858).

1759. The state of Europe: for three years Britain had been at war with France and was fighting at sea in America, in India, and—with Prussia as an ally—in Europe. This same year, after a period of reverses, brought several victories. Horace Walpole commented, 'We are forced to ask every morning what victory there is for fear of missing one.'

Moreover, in 1759, the British Museum was opened in January; in March Halley's comet was at its perihelion in the skies, having appeared as predicted by the astronomer Edmund

Halley who had died as long before this as 1742; in August was fought the Battle of Minden in which the Anglo-Hanoverian army defeated the French, while at sea Boscawen defeated the French fleet at Lagos; in September in Canada occurred the Battle of Quebec and the death of Wolfe after his complete victory over Montcalm who was also killed; in October the Eddystone Lighthouse was completed, while in an earthquake in Syria no fewer than twenty thousand people perished. In November there was another British naval victory over the French at Quiberon Bay, and Mount Vesuvius was in violent eruption. This was the year, too, of Voltaire's *Candide*, Dr. Johnson's *Rasselas*, and Joseph Haydn's very first Symphony.

In 1760 King George II died, and was succeeded by King George III, aged twenty-two. James Macpherson published his *Fragments of Ancient Poetry*, reputedly by Ossian, and Laurence Sterne gave the world his *Tristram Shandy*, one of the most original novels ever written.

In 1761 the new king was crowned, having married Princess Charlotte of Mecklenburg-Strelitz a fortnight earlier. An alliance was made between France and Spain, and Pitt resigned from the government over the conduct of the War. Macpherson produced *Fingal*, Rousseau his *Nouvelle Héloïse*, and the Scottish atheist-philosopher, David Hume, his *History of England*.

The year 1762 began with Britain declaring war against Spain, just by way of increasing the chaotic state of Europe. In Russia the Empress Catherine II succeeded her consort Czar Peter III who had been deposed and strangled.

In the first few weeks of 1763 the Treaty of Paris was signed by Britain, France, Spain, and Portugal, so ending the Seven Years War. Immediately afterwards Prussia and Austria made peace with the Treaty of Hubertusburg.

In the following year, 1764, the eight-year-old musician of genius Wolfgang Amadeus Mozart visited England in the course of his first professional tour of Europe. He was accompanied by his father, Leopold Mozart, and his eleven-year-old sister, Nannerl. They had taken a coach from Paris to Calais on the 10th of April, and they arrived in London, after an unpleasant crossing in a specially hired boat, the packet-boat being full, on the 22nd. The little family lodged above a hairdresser's in Cecil Court, St. Martin's Lane. As early in their stay as the 27th of the same month they obtained permission to present themselves at Court. Both the King and Queen Charlotte had a great love for music, and the Mozarts' reception at St. James's Palace was so warm and unceremonious that it cheered them greatly. They were invited again on May 19th to play to a small gathering from six till ten in the evening. The King asked the boy-wonder to play pieces by Handel and others at sight. Thereafter the boy accompanied the Queen in an aria on the organ, then played with a flautist, then finally improvised a new melody and harmony on the bass of a Handel air. Handel had been dead five years, but his music still dominated musical London.

The following year, 1765, found the Mozarts still in London, and when the father fell ill the child prodigy took to composing, his first symphony being written in a house in Ebury Street, which still is extant, bearing a plaque to this same effect. The child Mozart's single year in London did him—and London— far more good than the Seven Years' War did Europe. Within this twelvemonth the King had a two-months' illness which affected his reason. And among important books published were Thomas Percy's *Reliques of Ancient English Poetry* and William Blackstone's *Commentaries on the Laws of England.* It was in this year that the infant Burns had the first of his meagre schooling. This continued, under William Murdoch, throughout the year following—which gave the world Oliver Goldsmith's novel *The Vicar of Wakefield.* Murdoch himself has told the story of Burns's education:

'In the year 1767 Mr. Burnes quitted his mud edifice [the cottage at Alloway where Robert was born], and took possession of a farm (Mount Oliphant) . . . This farm being at a considerable distance from the school, the boys could not attend regularly . . .'

The poet's brother Gilbert narrates what happened in 1768:

'There being no school near us, and our little services being

C. De Carmontelle del. 1764.   *A. Schiffordok*

THE MOZART FAMILY IN LONDON

useful on the farm, my father undertook to teach us arithmetic in
the winter evenings, by candle-light, and in this way my two
elder sisters got all the education they received . . .'

Thereafter he gives a vivid glimpse of the kind of family it was:

'Murdoch came to spend a night with us (at Mount Oliphant), and to take his leave when he was about to go into Carrick. He brought us as a present and memorial of him, a small compendium of English Grammar, and (Shakespeare's) tragedy of *Titus Andronicus*, and by way of passing the evening, he began to read the play aloud. We were all attention for some time, till presently the whole party was dissolved in tears. A female in the play (I have but a confused remembrance of it) had her hands chopt off, and her tongue cut out, and was then insultingly desired to call for water to wash her hands. At this, in an agony of distress, we with one voice desired he would read no more. My father observed that if we would not hear it out, it would be needless to leave the play with us. Robert replied, that if it was left he would burn it. My father was going to chide him for this ungrateful return to his tutor's kindness, but Murdoch interfered, declaring that he liked to see so much sensibility . . .'

In this same year the Scottish explorer, James Bruce, set out to discover the source of the River Nile, and Captain Cook, who was to discover Australia and New Zealand, embarked on his first voyage of survey. In London in early December the Royal Academy was instituted with Sir Joshua Reynolds as its first President. James Boswell, who was never to meet Burns, published his *Journal of a Tour to Corsica*, and Francis Grose, who was to become an important friend of the poet's, published his *Dictionary of the Vulgar Tongue*.

The year 1769 brought important inventions: Richard Arkwright of Preston produced his spinning-frame which revolutionised the manufacture of cotton, and James Watt of Greenock invented his steam engine which was eventually to begin the railway system. Napoleon and Arthur Wellesley, later the great Duke of Wellington, were born. Nearer Burns's home the building of the New Town of Edinburgh began.

In 1770 Lord North became Prime Minister of Great Britain and Ireland; Captain Cook landed at Botany Bay and named New South Wales; Bruce reached the source of the Blue Nile; a panic at a fireworks display at Versailles killed nearly one thousand people; Beethoven was born at Bonn; and in Scotland agrarian improvements on a large scale began in Ayrshire. But Burns was still only a boy of eleven.

When the poet was twelve, in the following year, Arkwright established his first spinning-mill, Walter Scott was born in Edinburgh, and—also in Edinburgh—the *Encyclopaedia Britannica* was first published. So also was Henry Mackenzie's *The Man of Feeling* and Tobias George Smollett's *Humphrey Clinker,* Smollett dying this same year at Leghorn. Both of these latter authors became favourites of Burns as he grew older.

In 1772 both Robert and Gilbert Burns attended the parish school of Dalrymple near Ayr—taking week about because their hard-labouring father could not spare them both together. This arrangement lasted only for a quarterly term. Joseph Priestley, the great chemist of Leeds, discovered the composition of the atmosphere; but a serious dearth of oatmeal must have been a much more immediate preoccupation at Mount Oliphant.

In the autumn of 1773 Dr. Johnson and James Boswell set out on their tour of Scotland and the Hebrides, and came as near to Alloway as Auchinleck in the same county. In Boston, Mass., there happened the famous Tea Party; in Edinburgh there was opened the first deaf-and-dumb academy in Britain; and there appeared for the first time the *Poetical Works of Robert Fergusson,* the book that was to influence Burns's own poetry profoundly. Fergusson died the following year, aged only twenty-four.

In 1774 war broke out with the American colonists, Priestley discovered oxygen, the Register House was built in Edinburgh, and the rules of cricket were formulated by 'a committee of noblemen and gentlemen'. Burns, now fifteen, might be said to be finishing his much interrupted education, at Hugh Rodger's school at Kirkoswald. But he was intermittently labouring on his father's farm as well.

It was now, when he was not quite fifteen, that Burns produced his first poem, the song beginning 'O, once I lov'd a Bonie Lass'. It was inspired—if inspiration is the word for a not very promising lyric—by one Nelly Kirkpatrick, 'a bonie, sweet, sonsie lass' of fourteen who was the poet's neighbour in the harvest field.

His brother Gilbert vividly describes the conditions at Mount Oliphant, a farm where conditions refused to prosper:

'We lived very sparingly. For several years butcher's meat was a stranger in the house, while all the members of the family exerted themselves to the utmost of their strength, and rather beyond it, in the labours of the farm. My brother at the age of thirteen assisted in threshing the crop of corn, and at fifteen was the principal labourer on the farm, for we had no hired servant, male or female. The anguish of mind we felt at our tender years, under these straits and difficulties, was very great. To think of our father growing old (for he was now above fifty), broken down with the long continued fatigues of his life, with a wife and five other children, and in a declining state of circumstances, these reflections produced in my brother's mind and mine sensations of the deepest distress. I doubt not but the hard labour and sorrow of this period of his life, was in a great measure the cause of that depression of spirits with which Robert was so often afflicted through his whole life afterwards.'

In the wide world in this same year, 1775, the disastrous American war was in full swing, while in the small world of Ayrshire the castle at Culzean 'on Carrick shore' was being built for the Ailsa family by Robert Adam, certainly the greatest architect who ever left Scotland for London, with the possible exception of his brother James who did likewise.

The year 1776 brought the Declaration of American Independence on July 4th. It brought also the first publication of two striking and influential books—Adam Smith's *The Wealth of Nations* and the first volume of Edward Gibbon's *The Decline and Fall of the Roman Empire.*

In 1777 the Burns family moved from Mount Oliphant— where they had struggled and wrought hard for ten years—to another farm, Lochlie, in the parish of Tarbolton. William Burnes secured the lease from an Ayr merchant who helped to stock the farm. They were to stay here for four years which Burns himself described in the autobiographical letter to Dr. Moore:

'For four years we lived comfortably here; but a lawsuit between him [his father] and his Landlord commencing, after three years tossing and whirling in the vortex of Litigation, my father was just saved from absorption to a jail by phthisical consumption, which after two years' promises, kindly stept in and snatch'd him away—"To where the wicked cease from troubling, and where the weary be at rest".'

In this same year Dr. Dodd was publicly executed at Tyburn for the crime of forgery, and there were industrial or anti-machinery riots at Manchester. In London there was the production of Sheridan's masterpiece, *The School for Scandal*, and in Ayrshire Andrew Wright's first tour of the country to report the state of agriculture.

In 1778 France recognised the existence of the United States of America and declared war on Britain. John Paul Jones, the Scots-American privateer, threatened the Firth of Clyde. This

THE TWA BRIGS OF AYR

he did in a brig of eighteen guns, performing some daring exploits, including a descent on the Solway Firth. The year after, as commodore of a small French squadron flying American colours, he threatened Leith and later captured two British men-of-war off Flamborough Head. The French king, Louis XIV, created him a Chevalier of the Order of Military Merit. Ten years later he is heard of as rear-admiral of the Russian fleet in the Black Sea fighting the Turks. He was to die in Paris in 1792. His name curiously survives as that given to a dance in the modern dance-hall, though few of the dancers may know anything of his career or his character. He was a thorough seaman of ferocious courage and an out-and-out adventurer 'of excessive vanity and detestable moral character'.

In 1779 Burns became twenty years old and, directly against his father's wishes, had meanwhile been taking some dancing lessons: .

'My father was the sport of strong passions: from that instance of rebellion he took a kind of dislike to me which, I believe, was one cause of that dissipation which marked my future years—I only say, Dissipation, comparative with the strictness and sobriety of Presbyterean country life; for though the will-o'-wisp meteors of thoughtless Whim were almost the sole lights of my path, yet early ingrained Piety and Virtue never failed me out the line of Innocence.—The great misfortune of my life was—never to have AN AIM . . . Thus, abandoned of aim or view in life; with a strong appetite for sociability, as well from native hilarity as from a pride of observation and remark; a constitutional hypochondriac taint which made me fly solitude; add to all these incentives to social life, my reputation from bookish knowledge, a certain wild logical talent, and a strength of thought something like the rudiments of good sense, made me generally a welcome guest. So 'tis no great wonder that always where two or three were met together, there was I in the midst of them.'

He goes on from here to expatiate on his favourite subject—the joy he found then, and ever after in his life, among 'the lasses, O'.

This essential and ungainsayable aspect of Burns has been summed up better—with more sense and frankness—by Professor Daiches than by any other critic or biographer:

'Burns enjoyed sex with a huge enjoyment; it was for him one of the most exciting elements—perhaps *the* most exciting —in human experience, and while he explored its emotional aspects in some of the most tender and passionate love lyrics ever written, he also produced with equal gusto and with equal skill remarkable lyrical comments on the purely physical aspect of the relation between the sexes.'

In the year 1780 Burns celebrated his coming-of-age by helping to found the Tarbolton Bachelors' Club. The rules of this society probably, but not certainly, were drawn up by Burns himself, and they mirror his view of what constituted enjoyable behaviour, not to say good citizenship, for example:

'Every man proper for a member of this Society must have a frank, open, honest heart; above any thing dirty or mean; and must be a professed lover of one or more of the female sex. No haughty, self-conceited person, who looks upon himself as superior to the rest of the Club, and especially no mean-spirited worldly mortal, whose only will is to heap up money, shall upon any pretence whatever be admitted. In short, the proper person for this Society is—a cheerful, honest-hearted lad; who, if he has a friend that is true, and a mistress that is kind, and as much wealth as genteelly to make both ends meet— is just as happy as this world can make him.'

In this year there were anti-popery riots in Edinburgh, and in the year after there was a week of similar riots in London, the Gordon Riots. Internationally Britain was now at war with Spain and the Netherlands. It was in this year, too, the year of 1781, that Burns had a brief infatuation for Alison Begbie, the first lass to whom he ever proposed marriage, and who probably inspired his first really beautiful and inimitable song, *Mary Morison,* which is 'a gem of purest ray serene'. The relationship was broken off probably because Burns had been sent by his father to live for a space in Irvine, a town on the Ayrshire coast, and to learn the trade of flax-dressing. He spent there a few months of his young-manhood. On reaching the age of twenty-two his mind had turned seriously to thoughts of matrimony. This, he recognised, was impossible on his wages as a ploughman at Lochlie, a wage which never exceeded six or seven pounds a year. The additional piece of land—about three acres—which he and his brother Gilbert had rented from their father for the special cultivation of flax added little to their meagre fortune. It was Robert who had the idea to 'dress' the flax as well as raise it. The father, who had been thinking of giving over his whole farm to flax, readily acquiesced in Robert's scheme for learning flax-dressing.

Irvine at this time was a town much larger than Ayr and one of the principal centres of the flax-dressing industry in Scotland. Accordingly, and soon after Burns's initiation as a Freemason, he said a fond farewell to Alison Begbie and moved to Irvine to learn the new business of 'heckling', as it was called.

Manufacturing was not carried on at Irvine to any great extent when Burns went to stay there. The young men of the town were generally sailors, or went to the West Indies or America as planters and store-keepers. Many went also to the East Indies—some in the mercantile line, others in the military, and several of these returned to the town with quite considerable fortunes. One such was Captain Richard Brown whose remarkable acquaintance the poet was about to make. The numbers of incorporated trades in Irvine in the year 1781 were roughly as follows—weavers 116; shoemakers 56; blacksmiths 24; tailors 27; coopers 7; masons and wrights 80. Of other employment there were 10 maltsters, 6 butchers, 7 bakers, 6 clothiers, 2 chandlers, 6 barbers, 150 coal-hewers, 60 carters, 8 carriers, 2 saddlers, 3 coppersmiths, 2 druggists, 3 surgeons, and 1 physician. There was one whisky still, which consumed about 950 bolls of malt yearly. There was one small brewery, most of the ale being brewed by retailers themselves. Many private families brewed their own beer. Among the weavers were makers of muslin and silk gauze. A spinning-jenny had recently been erected which employed about 80 hands. Coal was a major export from Irvine harbour—about 24,000 tons annually. Considerable quantities of woollen carpets, muslins and silk stuffs, lawns, gauzes, and the linen known as Kenting were exported to Ireland. The chief articles of import were hemp, iron, timber from Memel and Norway, ship timber from Wales, raw hides, skins, and grain from Ireland, and from Ireland also came 10,000 quarters of grain in one year. The population of Irvine in the year of Burns's stay there was around 4,400.

In a contemporary report we learn that the inhabitants were social and cheerful, and seldom riotous. They are described as humane and hospitable and generous, 'though these qualities were not in every instance exerted with necessary prudence'—which is given as the reason why the streets were so much infested with vagrant poor.

On the first day of January, 1782, the shop in which Burns was learning to heckle flax was destroyed by fire, and shortly afterwards he returned to the farm at Lochlie. In the course of the same year Great Britain formally recognized the independence of the United States. It was a bad year for Scottish farmers. There were snowstorms before the harvest was reaped.

In the following year, 1783, the poet's unhappy father was engaged in tedious litigation over his tenanting of the farm at Lochlie. In the autumn Robert and Gilbert secretly planned to rent another farm at Mossgiel near Mauchline. In the greater world the Treaty of Versailles brought the European war to an end, being signed by Britain, France and Spain. The chemist Lavoisier in France discovered that water was a chemical combination of oxygen and hydrogen; and in London the inventor and ironmaster, Henry Cort, discovered the puddling-furnace method of manufacturing iron. By way of disaster no fewer than forty thousand people perished in an earthquake in Sicily.

In the January of 1784 the Court of Session upheld the appeal of William Burnes. But a fortnight later the poor man died and his family moved to Mossgiel. Meanwhile more than fifty people died of the smallpox in Irvine in this year. In England the first Methodist Conference was instituted by John Wesley. The great new tragédienne, Sarah Siddons, came direct from Drury Lane to overwhelm Edinburgh.

In May of the year 1785, Elizabeth Paton, a farm-servant at Lochlie, presented Robert with the first of his many illegitimate children. She was a plain girl with a good figure. Burns's mother wanted the poet to marry the girl, but brother Gilbert counselled him against it. Burns's sister Isabella described Elizabeth as 'rude and uncultivated to a great degree' and 'with a contempt for every sort of refinement', though allowing that the girl regarded Robert 'with a most beautiful devotion'. In his *Epistle to John Rankine,* Burns describes this wench as a partridge he had brought down with his gun. Much less coarse—indeed touching and charming—are the stanzas entitled *A Poet's Welcome to his Love-Begotten Daughter*. About a year later Elizabeth Paton issued a maintenance claim on Burns and was successfully fobbed off with twenty pounds which came out of the profits of the Kilmarnock edition of his poems.

Meanwhile, also in the year 1785, Burns wrote some of his best satires and his fantastic comic-opera, *The Jolly Beggars,* which both Stevenson and Carlyle rated above *Tam o'Shanter* itself and which Matthew Arnold was to describe as 'a splendid and puissant production'. He also finished his first *Commonplace Book*—a rag-bag of reflections written in his curiously stilted prose. And he first made the acquaintance of Jean Armour whom he was eventually to marry after long delays and the birth of two sets of twins born out of wedlock. In Europe and the world in general it was an uneventful year—its most delightful happening being the first production of Mozart's opera, *The Marriage of Figaro*. Here, in parenthesis, let me suggest that there is a strange parallelism—it has not, to my knowledge been pointed out before—between the careers of Mozart and Burns though, of course, the composer and the poet were never to meet. They were exact contemporaries; they both died in their late middle-thirties. In the pitifully short span of their worldly existence they both enriched humanity with their different arts, each in his own style and medium. They were both loveable young men, and both bright-eyed and not unduly conscience-ridden voluptuaries, and each in his sort spread all the happiness and gave all the joy he could to his fellow men—(and especially to his fellow women).

Early in 1786 Burns was planning to run away from it all by emigrating to Jamaica. In April Jean's father, James Armour, repudiated Burns as a son-in-law. He has been described as 'a rather dour, churchy man', and both he and his wife deplored their daughter's affair with Burns until—later in the same year— the young man found himself a famous poet. It was then that, newly returned from his Edinburgh triumph, the Armours treated Burns—rather to his disgust—with a 'new servility'. It was on the last day of July that the Kilmarnock edition of Burns's poems was published. He awoke, like Byron, to find himself famous, and the proposed emigration to Jamaica was first postponed and then abandoned. In September Jean

EDINBURGH

Armour bore him twins which were christened Robert and Jean. At the end of November the poet travelled to Edinburgh, and in December Henry Mackenzie, the Man of Feeling, gave high praise to his poems and an Edinburgh edition was proposed.

In 1787 the American Constitution was ratified, and a society was formed for the suppression of the Slave Trade. Schiller wrote *Don Carlos,* and Mozart composed *Don Giovanni.* And meanwhile, in Scotland, Don Giovanni Burns was having an *annus mirabilis.* In January the Grand Lodge of Scotland toasted him as Caledonia's Bard (he had become a Freemason at Tarbolton in 1781). On April 21st the Edinburgh edition of his poems was published, when he sold his copyright for one hundred guineas. For three weeks in May he toured the Scottish borders with his bosom-friend Robert Ainslie. In June he received an appeal from May Cameron, an Edinburgh servant-girl whom he had got with child. Burns at once wrote to Ainslie (who was in the same paternal predicament himself) asking him to 'send for the wench and give her ten or twelve shillings . . . and advise her out to some country friends . . . Call immediately, or at least as soon as it is dark, for God's sake, lest the poor soul be starving.' Most of Burns's biographers who go so far as to quote this do not go further and quote a revealing later remark in the same letter, which is a kind of flashlight on the pretty morals of these rustic cronies: 'But don't for Heaven's sake meddle with her as a Piece.'

A week later Burns made what he himself calls 'an eclatant return' to Mauchline. In June he toured the West Highlands as far as Inveraray, and at the end of July he describes Jean in one of his letters as being 'in for it again'—meaning, of course, pregnant. In August he completed his long and important autobiographical letter written to Dr. John Moore at the incitation of his affectionate but shockable friend, Mrs. Dunlop. On August 8th he returned to Edinburgh for three weeks, following this with three weeks of a Highland tour with his friend William Nicol. In October he toured in Stirlingshire where he received the news of the death of one of his twins, Jean. In December he first met Mrs. Agnes McLehose (Clarinda) and began his highly affected correspondence with her. But just as important as anything else in this important year was the appearance in May of the first volume of the *Scots Musical Museum*. This was originated by one James Johnson, and it was the exposition of an idea he had had of collecting the words and music of all the existing Scots songs and publishing them. By the time he met Burns his first volume—containing one hundred songs—was already in the press. He invited Burns to help him in the preparation of a second volume, and the poet's enthusiasm eventually outdid that of Johnson himself. Burns had no singing voice, but his knowledge of music was far greater than some of his biographers have suggested. Throughout their association Johnson always accepted Burns' superior taste and never questioned his advice.

On the 20th October of this same eventful year Burns told the Duke of Gordon's librarian, James Hoy, of his personal interest in the project:

'An engraver, James Johnson in Edinburgh has, not from mercenary views but from an honest Scotch enthusiasm, set about collecting all our native Songs and setting them to music; particularly those that have never been set before. Clarke, the well-known musician, presides over the musical arrangement; and Drs. Beattie and Blacklock, Mr. Tytler, Woodhouselee, and your humble servant to the utmost of his small power, assist in collecting the old poetry, or sometimes to a fine air to make a stanza, when it has no words.'

He began active work for the *Scots Musical Museum* in November. The project had his whole heart.

Thus in February of the following year, 1788, he wrote to his friend James Candlish:

'At present I have time for nothing. Dissipation and business engross every moment. I am engaged in assisting an honest Scots enthusiast, a friend of mine who is an Engraver, and has taken it unto his head to publish a collection of all our songs set to music, of which the words and music are done by Scotsmen.

This, you will easily guess, is an undertaking exactly to my taste.'

To Johnson himself Burns sent one of his 'regular bounder' letters announcing his marriage to Jean Armour in May, 1788. This is what he wrote:

'I am so enamoured with a certain girl's prolific twin-bearing merit, that I have given her a *legal* title to the best blood in my body; and so farewell Rakery!'

What a man! At the beginning of this same year the affair with Clarinda was at its height and the poet on one occasion sent her four fancy letters within two days. In March, his Jean presented him with two twin girls, one of whom lived only for a week while the other lived less than three weeks. In late April he acknowledged Jean Armour as his wife. Yet in November an Edinburgh wench called Jenny Clow bore him a son. Burns said he would take the child into his own home, but Jenny refused to part with him. Jenny appears to have been formerly Clarinda's maid. Burns wrote to Clarinda asking her to get a porter to take five shillings from the poet to Jenny! What we are bound to call brazen caddishness could hardly go further. In March appeared the second volume of the *Scots Musical Museum,* and in June the poet and his patient prolific Jean moved to what was to be the last of his farm-buildings, Ellisland near Dumfries.

On the 1st of January of this same year, 1788, there appeared in London the first issue of *The Times* newspaper. At the end of the same month died the Young Pretender, Bonnie Prince

Charlie, in exile and decay. February brought the impeachment of Warren Hastings and the beginning of his trial, which was to last seven years. On the 1st October Deacon Brodie was executed in Edinburgh—hanged for burglary. On the 12th it became general knowledge that the King, George III, was insane. In Germany Goethe published his *Egmont*, and in England Jeremy Bentham gave the world his *Principles of Morals and Legislation*.

1789 was the year of the mutiny of the *Bounty*, the year when George Washington was elected first President of the United States, and the first year of the French Revolution, the Bastille being taken and destroyed by a bloodthirsty mob on July 14th. On January 31st the Prince of Wales accepted the Regency on the Government's terms. On August 4th the French National Assembly issued the Declaration of the Rights of Man. And in London a unique poet, William Blake, published his *Songs of Innocence*.

In February our own poet was in Edinburgh for twelve days, closing his accounts with his publisher, William Creech, and also settling Jenny Clow's suit. This summer, too, he first met Captain Grose, the antiquarian and scholar; and in August Mrs. Burns presented him with a son, a legitimate one by way of change. On September 1st the poet began in his post of Excise Officer since he could not make the Ellisland farm yield him an adequate living. In the winter, too, he suffered a serious illness described by himself as 'malignant squinancy and low fever'.

In 1790 Goethe published his *Faust* and Edmund Burke his *Reflections on the French Revolution*. In February in London the new newspaper, *The Times*, ran into trouble for printing libels on the Royal Family. It was fined two hundred pounds and the printer was imprisoned for a year. In the same month appeared the third volume of the *Scots Musical Museum* with many contributions by Burns. To this year we owe *Tam o' Shanter*, which was written at white heat in the course of one afternoon at Ellisland.

On March 31st of the following year, 1791, Anne Park of the Globe Tavern in Dumfries presented Burns with an illegitimate daughter, while nine days later Jean gave him another legitimate son. In March *Tam o' Shanter* was published in the *Edinburgh Magazine,* and the same masterpiece appeared in Grose's *Antiquities of Scotland* in April. In the autumn Burns auctioned his crops at Ellisland and renounced his lease of the farm. In November he moved to Dumfries, and in the first fortnight in December he was in Edinburgh again saying more fond farewells to Clarinda. Abroad the French king, Louis XVI, was arrested at Varennes on his flight from Paris; and the heaven-sent composer Mozart died at the age of thirty-five and was buried in a pauper's grave. His last opera, *The Magic Flute,* was performed for the first time; and in London there was published James Boswell's great biography of Dr. Samuel Johnson.

Among the news items in the year 1792 is one to remind us that we are still in the eighteenth century. In March the King of Sweden was assassinated by one Count Anherstrom. By way of punishment the Count was scourged with whips of iron thongs, had his right hand cut off, then his head, then he was impaled. In August the French royal family was imprisoned, and in the following month came the ghastly September massacres. In the same year, though, came enlightenment in a different sense. An Ayrshireman, William Murdoch—born at Auchinleck—who was a distinguished and versatile scientist, made the discovery of coal-gas as a means of illumination, though he did not succeed in making it practical until ten years had elapsed. And Edinburgh opened its first school for the blind.

There was a strong whiff of liberty in the air of these rapidly changing times, and Burns savoured it as much as any of his countrymen. Almost the most significant event of the year was the publication of Thomas Paine's *The Rights of Man,* the work of a demagogue of something like genius. I cannot trace any evidence of Burns's having read this inflammatory book; but it certainly voiced many of his own sentiments and convictions. The book was a reply to Burke's *Reflections on the French Revolution,* and Paine had an advantage over Burke in that he took an active part in the revolutionary movement in America (1774–1787) and later went to France to fall foul of Robespierre because of a plan he had of letting the French king escape to America.

The fourth volume of the *Scots Musical Museum* was published in this year, and Burns became interested in a similar project, George Thomson's *Select Collection of Scottish Airs*. Burns agreed to help in this publication, but with a stubbornness which is hard to understand he refused remuneration—even though he was poorly off as always, and had an almost alarmingly growing family. He wrote these words to Thomson:

'As to my remuneration, you may think my Songs either *above* or *below* price; for they shall absolutely be the one or the other. In the honest enthusiasm with which I embark on your undertakings, to talk of money, wages, fee, hire, etc., could be downright Sodomy of Soul!'

This feeling, so singularly expressed, is surely proof of a foolhardiness which the poet himself mistook for pride. Burns's first biographer, by the way, the egregious Dr. James Currie, took the liberty of substituting the word Prostitution for the word Sodomy, thereby revealing what Maurice Lindsay has called 'a nice sense of moral distinction'.

For his first instalment of twenty-five songs Burns received, against his will and his stipulation, a five-pound note from Thomson. He wrote an angry letter of protest saying he would terminate the contract at once if Thomson ever sent money again. He swallowed the insult—'To return it would savour of bombast affectation.' And then he goes on in a style for which bombast affectation is just about the best possible description:

'Burns's character for Generosity of Sentiment, and Independence of Mind, will, I trust, long outlive any of his wants which the cold, unfeeling, dirty Ore can supply . . .'

Thomson, very naturally, never tried to repeat his gesture until a few days before Burns's death when, in an agony of desperation, the poet had to write begging him for a further five pounds. He had gone on supplying Thomson with songs in the interval.

Burns easily restores himself to his usual likeableness in a long letter to Thomson describing the deep pleasure he got from fitting lyrics to the beloved old tunes he knew by heart:

'When I feel my Music beginning to jade, I retire to the solitary fireside of my study, and there commit my effusions to paper; swinging, at intervals, on the hind-leg of my elbow-chair, by way of calling forth my own critical strictures, as my pen goes.'

In November of that year the willing and fecund Mrs. Burns gave her indefatigable spouse another daughter, whom they named Elizabeth.

Very early in the year 1793 we find Burns in some trouble for uttering republican sentiments—trouble he certainly asked for since as an exciseman he was a government official. In February the second Edinburgh edition of his poems was published, and in June the first number of Thomson's *Select Collection*. Meanwhile Burns and family moved into the still-extant house in Mill Vennel, Dumfries, where he spent his last three years on earth. At the end of July he went on a three-day walking tour in Galloway with his friend John Syme, who was kind to Burns in his last illness and has left a vivid and not-too-well-known description of the poet's physical features:

'The poet's expression varied perpetually, according to the idea that predominated in his mind; and it was beautiful to remark how well the play of his lips indicated the sentiment he was about to utter. His eyes and lips, the first remarkable for fire, and the second for flexibility, formed at all times an index to his mind, and as sunshine or shade predominated, you might have told *a priori,* whether the company was to be favoured with a scintillation of wit, or a sentiment of benevolence, or a burst of fiery indignation . . . I cordially concur with what Sir Walter Scott says of the poet's eyes. In his animated moments, and particularly when his anger was aroused by instances of tergiversation, meanness or tyranny, they were actually like coals of living fire.'

In January of this year the King of France was guillotined. The whole of Europe including Britain was up in arms against that seething country. In April the Committee of Public Safety

was established and took control. In July Marat was stabbed
to death, and in October the Queen, Marie Antoinette, was
guillotined.

At the turn of the year there happened the notorious episode
involving the Riddell family who had been kind and hospitable
to the poet. But on one occasion—the whole business is involved
and much obscured by legend—it seems certain that Burns
behaved like a boor with his hostess, exposed his strength as
well as his weakness, wrote a letter of semi-jocose apology and
mock-despair, and was not answered or ever forgiven. In August
of the same year, 1794, Jean gave him another son.

The outer world was in a ferment likewise. In Poland there
was a rising which the Scottish poet Thomas Campbell (who
attended Burns's funeral as a boy) immortalised in a single
marvellous couplet:

> 'Hope, for a season, bade the world farewell,
> And Freedom shrieked—as Kosciusko fell!'

And in France the execution of Danton in April and of
Robespierre in July brought an end to the Reign of Terror.

The year 1795 was comparatively uneventful if we except the
Prince Regent's marriage to Princess Caroline of Brunswick
and the emergence of young Napoleon Buonaparte to save the
French Government by 'a whiff of grapeshot'. Burns's republican
sentiments and utterance now got him into more trouble since
they alienated him from his valuable and influential friend,
Mrs. Dunlop, who had befriended him loyally for nearly ten
years. In September his little daughter Elizabeth died, and in
the winter he himself was laid low with rheumatic fever.

In January of 1796, which was to be the year of his death,
the poet wrote to Mrs. Dunlop seeking a reconciliation:

'Will you be so obliging, dear Madam, as to condescend on
that my offence which you seem determined to punish with a
deprivation of that friendship which once was the source of
my highest enjoyments? Alas! Madam, ill can I afford, at this
time to be deprived of any of the small remnant of my pleasures.
I have lately drank deep of the cup of affliction. [Then note

how the genuine feeling seeps through the stilted verbiage.]
The autumn robbed me of my only daughter and darling child—
and that at a distance too and so rapidly as to put it out of my
power to pay the last duties to her. I had scarcely begun to
recover from that shock, when I became myself the victim of a
most severe rheumatic fever, and long the die spun doubtful;
until after many weeks of a sick-bed it seems to have turned up
more life, and I am beginning to crawl across my room, and
once indeed have been before my own door in the street.'

But the 'more life' was to last for only six months.

It is good to know that Burns read and relished a note of
reconciliation from Mrs. Dunlop on his death-bed. This was in
the summer of the year 1796. In July he spent his ghastly fortnight on the Solway coast, where, following the advice of an
idiotic doctor, he took a course of sea-bathing to cure his
rheumatic fever. He returned to Dumfries, mortally sick, on the
16th of July and he died on the 21st.

In 1824 Allan Cunningham wrote eloquently about Burns's
death and funeral in the *London Magazine:*

'I went to see him laid out for the grave, several elder people
with me. He lay in a plain unadorned coffin, with a linen sheet
drawn over his face, and on the bed, and around the body,
herbs and flowers were thickly strewn, according to the usage of
the country. He was wasted somewhat by long illness; but
death had not increased the swarthy hue of his face, which
was uncommonly dark and deeply marked—his broad and open
brow was pale and serene, and around it his sable hair lay in
masses, slightly touched with grey . . . The multitude who
accompanied Burns to the grave went step by step with the
chief mourners. They might amount to ten or twelve thousand.
Not a word was heard . . . It was an impressive and mournful
sight to see men of all ranks and persuasions and opinions
mingling as brothers, and stepping side by side down the streets
of Dumfries, with the remains of him who had sung of their loves
and joys and domestic endearments, with a truth and a tenderness which none perhaps have since equalled.'

THE WORDSWORTHS VISIT ELLISLAND

6 · *Views from Home and Abroad*

HEAR Walt Whitman in *November Boughs*, 1886–1888:

'Dear Bob! Manly, witty, fond, friendly, full of weak spots as well as strong ones—essential type of so many thousands—perhaps the average, as just said, of the decent-born young men and the early mid-aged, not only of the British Isles, but America, too, North and South, just the same. I think, indeed, one best part of Burns is the unquestionable proof he presents of the perennial existence among the laboring classes, especially farmers, of the finest latent poetic elements in their blood . . . Perhaps no one ever sang "lads and lassies"—that universal race, mainly the same, too, all ages, all lands—down on their own plane, as he has. He exhibits no philosophy worth mentioning; his mortality is hardly more than parrot-talk—not bad or deficient, but cheap, shopword, the platitudes of old aunts and uncles to the youngsters (be good boys and keep your noses clean). Only when he gets at Poosie Nansie's, celebrating the "barley bree", or among tramps, or democratic bouts and

WALT WHITMAN

drinking generally ("Freedom and whisky gang thegither"),
we have, in his own unmistakable color and warmth, those
interiors of rake-helly life and tavern fun—the cantabile of
jolly beggars in highest jinks—lights and groupings or rank glee
and brawny amorousness, outvying the best painted pictures of
the Dutch school, or any school . . . The aforesaid "odd-kind
chiel" remains to my heart and brain as almost the tenderest,
manliest, and (even if contradictory) dearest flesh-and-blood
figure in all the streams and clusters of by-gone poets.'

And hear another transatlantic and equally unfamiliar view-
point. It is by an American writer much more revered than
Whitman:

'He has given voice to all the experiences of common life, he has endeared the farm-house and cottage, patches and poverty, beans and barley; ale, the poor man's wine; hardship; the fear of debt; the dear society of weans and wife, of brothers and sisters, proud of each other, knowing so few, and finding amends for want and obscurity in books and thoughts . . . As he was thus the poet of the poor, anxious, cheerful, working humanity, so had he the language of low life. He grew up in a rural district, speaking a *patois* so unintelligible to all but natives, and he has made the Lowland Scotch a Doric dialect of fame. *It is the only example in history of a language made classic by the genius of a single man,'* [Italics mine!]

So spoke the American, Ralph Waldo Emerson, at a Burns Centenary address at Boston in 1859.

RALPH WALDO EMERSON

And then there is Longfellow, whose handsome poem in the Burns style is undeservedly little known:

> I see amid the fields of Ayr
> A ploughman who in foul or fair
>   Sings at his task,
> So clear we know not if it is
> The laverock's song we hear or his,
>   Nor care to ask.
>
> For him the ploughing of those fields
> A more ethereal harvest yields
>   Than sheaves of grain:
> Songs flush with purple bloom the rye;
> The plover's call, the curlew's cry,
>   Sing in his brain.
>
> Touched by his hand, the wayside weed
> Becomes a flower; the lowliest reed
>   Beside the stream
> Is clothed with beauty; gorse and grass
> And heather, where his footsteps pass,
>   The brighter seem.
>
> He sings of love, whose flame illumes
> The darkness of lone cottage rooms;
>   He feels the force,
> The treacherous under-tow and stress,
> Of wayward passions, and no less
>   The keen remorse.
>
> At moments, wrestling with his fate,
> His voice is harsh, but not with hate;
>   The brushwood hung
> Above the tavern door lets fall
> Its bitter leaf, its drop of gall,
>   Upon his tongue.

HENRY WADSWORTH LONGFELLOW

But still the burden of his song
Is love of right, disdain of wrong;
    Its master chords
Are Manhood, Freedom, Brotherhood;
Its discords but an interlude
    Between the words.

And then to die so young, and leave
Unfinished what he might achieve!
    Yet better sure
Is this than wandering up and down,
An old man, in a country town,
    Infirm and poor.

> For now he haunts his native land
> As an immortal youth; his hand
>   Guides every plough;
> He sits beside each ingle-nook;
> His voice is in each rushing brook,
>   Each rustling bough.
>
> His presence haunts this room to-night,
> A form of mingled mist and light,
>   From that far coast.
> Welcome beneath this roof of mine!
> Welcome! this vacant chair is thine,
>   Dear guest and ghost!

Longfellow's exquisite imitation is also exquisite flattery.

In the same centenary year, and on the same occasion, the lovely Mrs. Caroline Norton—the model for Meredith's Diana of the Crossways—had turned out an occasional poem with couplets like this:

> Poet and man (not angel!),—earth to earth!—
> Dead are thy days of sorrow and of mirth.

She visited Edinburgh to celebrate the centenary and wrote to a friend:

'I missed the Ayr dinner, which I intended to have contemplated, by catching a cold walking in the wind and rain, in petticoats as short as Tam o' Shanter's Witch's sark . . . Edinburgh was very quiet on the Centenary day. Even the enthusiasm of the Scotch is *frappé à la glace*. It is a new acquaintance—and they don't feel familiar enough with it to be jolly. And think of three thousand sitting down to Temperance tea-trays! I'd as lief be a duck and sit in a pond with my chin upon duckweed!'

Equally ill-known, though much more accessible, are two poems by Wordsworth, apparently written on two consecutive days during the tour of Scotland in 1803, only seven years after Burns's death. The one is entitled *At the Grave of Burns, Seven*

THE LOVELY MRS. NORTON

Years After His Death, and the other, *Thoughts—Suggested the Day Following, on the Banks of Nith, near the Poet's Residence.* The first poem, written in the 'Burns Stanza', as indeed is the second, begins impressively:

> I shiver, Spirit fierce and bold,
> At thought of what I now behold:
> As vapours breathed from dungeon cold
>   Strike pleasure dead,
> So sadness comes from out the mould
>   Where Burns is laid.

There follow two stanzas of somewhat charnel moralising, whereafter the poet shakes himself free from convention and sighs over the fact that he might easily have met Burns and been his friend:

Fresh as the flower, whose modest worth
He sang, his genius, 'glinted' forth,
Rose like a star that touching earth,
   For so it seems,
Doth glorify its humble birth
   With matchless beams.

The piercing eye, the thoughtful brow,
The struggling heart, where be they now?—
Full soon the Aspirant of the plough,
   The prompt, the brave,
Slept with the obscurest, in the low
   And silent grave.

I mourned with thousands, but as one
More deeply grieved, for He was gone
Whose light I hailed when first it shone
   And showed my youth
How Verse may build a princely throne
   On humble truth.

Alas! where'er the current tends,
Regret pursues and with it blends—
Huge Criffel's hoary top ascends
   By Skiddaw seen,—
Neighbours we were, and loving friends
   We might have been;

True friends, though diversely inclined;
But heart with heart and mind with mind,
Where the main fibres are entwined,
   Through Nature's skill,
May even by contraries be joined
   More closely still.

The tear will start, and let it flow;
Thou 'poor Inhabitant below',
At this dread moment—even so—
   Might we together

Have sate and talked where gowans blow,
  Or on wild heather.

What treasures would have then been placed
Within my reach; of knowledge graced
By fancy what a rich repast!
  But why go on?—
Oh! spare to sweep, thou mournful blast,
  His grave grass-grown.

Wordsworth then sinks again, for three further stanzas, into funerary moralising, and he concludes his poem most piously:

Sighing, I turned away; but ere
Night fell I heard, or seemed to hear,
Music that sorrow comes not near,
  A ritual hymn,
Chanted in love that casts out fear
  By Seraphim.

Wordsworth's second Burns-inspired poem, again in the difficult Burns-stanza form, begins movingly and finely:

Too frail to keep the lofty vow
That must have followed when his brow
Was wreathed—'The Vision' tells us how—
  With holly spray,
He faltered, drifted to and fro,
  And passed away.

The next two stanzas reveal that Wordsworth and Dorothy—he apostrophises her as 'dear Sister'—had been indulging in 'social grief' on the subject of the departed poet, and that they had now travelled from Dumfries to the farm at Ellisland where he wrote *Tam o' Shanter*. But then the mood of mourning changes to a brighter hue:

Enough of sorrow, wreck, and blight;
Think rather of those moments bright
When to the consciousness of right
 His course was true,
When Wisdom prospered in his sight
 And virtue grew.

Yes, freely let our hearts expand,
Freely as in youth's season bland,
When side by side, his Book in hand,
 We wont to stray,
Our pleasure varying at command
 Of each sweet Lay.

How oft inspired must he have trod
These pathways, yon far-stretching road!
There lurks his home; in that Abode
 With mirth elate,
Or in his nobly-pensive mood
 The Rustic sate.

Proud thoughts that Image overawes,
Before it humbly let us pause,
And ask of Nature from what cause
 And by what rules
She trained her Burns to win applause
 That shames the Schools.

From there to the end the poem catches fire and ends in a blaze
of glory and grace, suggesting that Wordsworth's pen, as was its
not infrequent custom, ran away with him making him write
even better than he knew:

Through busiest street and loneliest glen
Are felt the flashes of his pen;
He rules mid winter snows, and when
 Bees fill their hives;
Deep in the general heart of men
 His power survives.

What need of fields in some far clime
Where Heroes, Sages, Bards sublime
And all that fetched the flowing rhyme
    From genuine springs,
Shall dwell together till old Time
    Folds up his wings?

Sweet Mercy! to the gates of Heaven
This Minstrel lead, his sins forgiven;
The rueful conflict, the heart riven
    With vain endeavour,
And memory of Earth's bitter leaven,
    Effaced for ever.

But why to Him confine the prayer,
When kindred thoughts and yearnings bear
On the frail heart the purest share
    With all that live?—
The best of what we do and are,
    Just God, forgive!

A third poem, again in the Burns stanza, is addressed *To the Sons of Burns* and is less worthy and distinctly patronising in tone:

For honest men delight will take
To spare your feelings for his sake,
Will flatter you, —and fool and rake
    Your steps pursue;
And of your Father's name will make
    A snare for you.

Wordsworth's sensitive sister, Dorothy, has in her Journal this entry for August 18th, 1803:

'We turned again to Burns's house. Mrs. Burns was gone to spend some time by the seashore with her children. We spoke to the servant-maid at the door, who invited us forward, and we sate down in the parlour. The walls were coloured with a blue wash; on one side of the fire was a mahogany desk, opposite to the window a clock, and over the desk a print from *Cotter's Saturday Night,* which Burns mentions in one of his letters having received as a present. The house was cleanly and neat in the inside, the stairs of stone scoured white, the kitchen on the right side of the passage, the parlour on the left. In the room above the parlour the poet died, and his son after him in the same room.'

On the same lines of high appreciation—though, of course, much later—is a passage in the works of that half-forgotten, wholly brilliant, literary and dramatic critic, George H. Mair, of the old *Manchester Guardian*. In his heyday, in the year 1911, he produced a little book entitled *English Literature*. This covers the subject in five hundred pages. Yet he devoted five of his most concentrated pages to an appraisal of Burns:

'Localized literatures rarely become known to the outside world, though their existence and probably some special knowledge of one or other of them is within the experience of most of us. But every now and again some one of their authors transcends his local importance, gives evidence of a genius which is not to be denied even by those who normally have not the knowledge to appreciate the particular flavour of locality which his writings impart, and becomes a national figure. While he lives and works the national and his local stream turn and flow together.

'This was the case of Robert Burns. All his life long he was the singer of a parish—the last of a long line of "forbears" who had used the Scottish lowland vernacular to rhyme in about their neighbours and their scandals, their loves and their church. Himself at the confluence of the two streams, the national and the local, he pays his tribute to two sets of originals, talks with equal reverence of names known to us like Pope and Gray and Shenstone and names unknown which belonged to local "bards", as he would have called them, who wrote their poems for an Ayrshire public. If he came upon England as an innovator it was simply because he brought with him the highly individualized style of Scottish local vernacular verse; to his own people he was no innovator but a fulfilment; as his best critic, W. E. Henley, says, he brought nothing to the literature he became a part of but himself. His daring and splendid genius made the local universal, raised out of rough and cynical satirizing a style as rich and humorous and astringent as that of Rabelais, lent inevitableness and pathos and romance to lyric and song. But he was content to better the work of other men. He made hardly anything new.

'Stevenson in his essay on Burns remarks his readiness to use up the work of others or take a large hint from it "as if he had some difficulty in commencing". He omits to observe that the very same trait applies to other great artists. There seem to be two orders of creative artists. On the one hand are the innovators, the new men like Blake, Wordsworth, Byron and Shelley, and later Browning. These men owe little to their predecessors; they work on their own devices and construct their medium afresh for themselves. Commonly their fame and acceptance is slow, for they speak in an unfamiliar tongue and they have to educate a generation to understand their work. The other order of artists have to be shown the way. They have little fertility in construction or invention. You have to say to them "Here is something that you could do too; go and do it better", or "Here is a story to work on, or a refrain of a song; take it and give it your subtlety, your music." The villainy you teach them they will use and it will go hard with them if they do not better the invention; but they do not invent for themselves. To this order of artists Burns like Shakespeare, and among the lesser men, Tennyson, belongs.'

Only a Scot—and Mair hailed from Aberdeen—would have the temerity to drag Tennyson into the argument. But he is too good a writer to be interrupted:

'In all his plays Shakespeare is known to have invented only one plot; in many he is using not only the structure but in many places the words devised by an older author; his mode of treatment depends on the conventions common in his day, on the tragedy of blood, and madness and revenge, on the comedy of intrigue and disguises, on the romance with its strange happenings and its reuniting of long-parted friends.

'Burns goes the same way to work; scarcely a page of his but shows traces of some original in the Scottish vernacular school. The elegy, the verse epistle, the satirical form of *Holy Willie's Prayer,* the song and recitative of *The Jolly Beggars,* are all to be found in his predecessors, in Fergusson, Ramsay, and the local poets of the south-west of Scotland. In the songs often whole verses, nearly always the refrains, are from older folk poetry. What he did was to pour into these forms the incomparable richness òf a personality whose fire and brilliance and humour transcended all locality and all tradition, a personality which strode like a colossus over the formalism and correctness of his time. His use of familiar forms explains, more than anything else, his immediate fame. His countrymen were ready for him; they could hail him on the instant (just as an Elizabethan audience could hail Shakespeare) as something familiar and at the same time more splendid than anything they knew. He spoke in a tongue they could understand.

'It is impossible to judge Burns from his purely English verse; though he did it as well as any of the minor followers of the school of Pope, he did it no better. Only the weakest side of his character —his sentimentalism—finds expression in it; he had not the sense of tradition nor the intimate knowledge necessary to use English to the highest poetic effect; it was indeed a foreign tongue to him. In the vernacular he wrote the language he spoke, a language whose natural force and colour had become enriched by three centuries of literary use, which was capable, too, of effects of humour and realism impossible in any tongue spoken out of reach of the soil. It held within it an unmatched faculty for pathos, a capacity for expressing a lambent and kindly humour, a power of pungency in satire and a descriptive vividness that English could not give . . .

'It is easy to see that though Burns admired unaffectedly the "classic" writers, his native realism and his melody made him a potent agent in the cause of naturalism and romance. In his ideas, even more than in his style, he belongs to the oncoming school. The French Revolution, which broke upon Europe when he was at the height of his career, found him already converted to its principles. As a peasant, particularly a Scottish peasant, he believed passionately in the native worth of man as man and gave ringing expression to it in his verse. In his youth his liberal-mindedness made him a Jacobite out of mere antagonism to the existing regime; the Revolution only discovered for him the more logical Republican creed. As the leader of a loose-living, hard-drinking set, such as was to be found in every parish, he was a determined and free-spoken enemy of the kirk, whose tyranny he several times encountered. In his writing he is as vehement an anti-clerical as Shelley and much more practical. The political side of romanticism, in fact, which in England had to wait for Byron and Shelley, is already full-grown in his work. He anticipates and gives complete expression to one half of the Romantic movement.'

Another *Manchester Guardian* man, the superb dramatic critic, C. E. Montague, had an appreciation of Burns as artist which is evinced in a letter to his elder brother, F. F. Montague, and is quoted at length in Oliver Elton's *Memoir*. The letter is dated February 16th, 1911:

'You amaze me by overlooking the structural cunning of Shakespeare's lyrics; and, as for *Tam o' Shanter* it has, *me iudice,* almost as much structure as a boat or a barrel, or a good vase, or his own *Jolly Beggars,* or a sonnet by Keats or any of the most finished structures there are. I remember you used to admire the structure of *Tom Jones,* but it seems to me, good as it is, to be almost top-heavy and lop-eared compared with the crafty distribution and balance of parts in *Tam o' Shanter,* and the "cuteness" of the dovetailings between, for instance, the narration and the reflective passages.'

Another writer who thought for himself in his approach to Burns is Professor Sir Walter Raleigh. He pointed out that the reason Wordsworth understood Burns so well was that he understood the inordinate excitements which beset the poetic temperament. Of *The Idiot Boy,* which even the avid Wordsworthian does not take at all seriously, Wordsworth himself wrote 'I never wrote anything with so much glee', and reminding us of this Raleigh goes on: 'In his search for the spirit of pleasure wherever it can be found, he readily accepts the felicities of love and wine.'

Oddly enough Raleigh overlooks a great poet—John Keats— whose soul was in some ways even more kindred to Burns's than was that of Wordsworth, and whose excitement at visiting Burns's native county is manifested in his letters if not so much in his poetry. But Raleigh certainly does not overlook the great Scottish sage who was born in Dumfriesshire, where Burns died: 'Carlyle knew poverty—the poverty that weighed on Burns from the cradle to the grave; he knew, also, and valued, the matchless sincerity of the man who speaks truly of human errors because he speaks mainly of his own.'

But Raleigh also shows himself out of sympathy with certain disparagers whose names are just as celebrated. With Arnold, for example: 'Matthew Arnold, who hated all that is national, brought a charge of provincialism against the poetry of Burns, which deals perpetually, he says, with Scotch drink, Scotch religion, and Scotch manners. If he added, as in fairness he should have added, that it deals with Scotch love, the fallacy would have been apparent.' Raleigh might here have added that Arnold certainly sensed the power and excitement of *Tam o' Shanter* and that he also—rather surprisingly—declared *The Jolly Beggars* to be a 'splendid and puissant production'.

Raleigh puts Stevenson in his place also:

'Robert Louis Stevenson, who had in him something of the Shorter Catechist, never showed it more clearly than when, from a boastful phrase of Burns in a letter to a boon companion, he elaborated his picture of the Old Hawk, the cold-blooded seducer of women.'

But surely 'hot-blooded' would have been an epithet nearer the truth? And another of the critics criticised was Henley, who was still alive when Raleigh wrote his essay:

'Mr. W. E. Henley wrote an essay on Burns which is a noble piece of English, and a brave counterblast to the Presbyterian apologists, but it is far too simple and clear-cut in its judgments.

"This lewd, amazing peasant of genius", is what he calls the poet; and though there is some truth in each of the epithets, they do not together make for intimacy and a sympathetic understanding. They are missiles, not discoveries. We are invited to go shares with the critic in his wonder, and in his social and moral censures. But these alien emotions are not what have given Burns his truest friends and disciples. Those who love him best do not wonder at him at all. He seems to them as obvious and natural as breathing. They think and feel what he thinks and feels; but he says more than they are in the habit of saying, and says it brilliantly. He is the voice of a million inarticulate consciences, who, if it were required of them, would cheerfully sign all that he says, and, in so doing, would be signing nothing that they do not understand and believe.'

This is incomparably well said, and the best explanation I have met with in all my reading of the reason why Burns means more to the Scot—far more, and to the unlettered Scot as well as to the lettered one, than Cervantes means to the Spaniard, Dante to the Italian, Goethe to the German, or Shakespeare to the Englishman. This is not to say that Burns is as great a writer as any of those four great ones (though the unlettered Scot would be willing to argue that he is). It is only to declare that Burns is himself a Scot in all his heart and soul and therefore addresses himself more directly to his countrymen than any of those great ones can do or ever try to do. (Parenthetically, may I state here that the fundamental difference between Scotland and England is that the Scot clamantly and never-endingly declares himself to be the Lord of Creation whereas the Englishman, quietly and unostentiously, knows that *he* is?)

Raleigh says something else that has not been said elsewhere, or at least not said so well:

'The Scottish people feel a hearty, instinctive, and just dislike for biographers of Burns. The life of Burns, full as it was of joy and generous impulse, full also of error, disappointment, and failure, makes a perfectly devised trap for the superior person. Almost everyone is superior to Robert Burns in some one point or other—in conjugal fidelity, in worldly prudence, or in social standing. Let him be careful to forget his advantages before he approaches this graveside, or his name will be added to the roll of the failures.'

But one of the poet's major virtues was that he was ever ready to be frank and unsparing about his own character, and here his ablest critic quotes him with a clinching effectiveness:

> O ye douce folk that live by rule,
> Grave, tideless-blooded, calm an' cool,
> Compar'd wi' you—O fool! fool! fool!
>   How much unlike!
> Your hearts are just a standing pool,
>   Your lives, a dyke!

It is because he understands both extremes—that of pleasure and that of prudence—that Burns is the national poet of Scotland and its people. This cool detached professor becomes warm and involved in his elaboration of this fact:

'That fierce and strenuous race has now for many centuries been divided into two irreconcilable parties. There is no gaiety in their religion, and very little sobriety in their pleasures. To this day, in any Scottish town, the inhabitants, who have worked together all the week, sort themselves out on the morning of Sunday, and make two parties, the sheep and the goats, each with its appropriate employ. The parties are mutually critical and mutually defiant, so that their differences are hardened by opposition. Innocent pleasures are driven into wild and violent courses, and become disreputable; piety and religion refuse all traffic with human weakness, and become grim and forbidding. If statistics could be compiled, it would probably be found that, in proportion to the number of the population, there are more fanatically righteous, and more dissolute, persons in Scotland than in any other country of Europe. Burns is the bard of both sects, and is enthusiastically accepted by both as their priest and prophet.'

He goes on, giving instances, to show how Burns could write

poetry profound in its intelligence and its piety and could also write ditties of so grotesque and so gargantuan a humour that they 'put to shame the lubricity and flatness of uninspired obscenity'. (It is more than doubtful whether Raleigh would call the recently published *Merry Muses*—previously only printed privately—anything better than uninspired obscenity). Burns, similarly, could express the constancy of settled love in one song, and glorify the transports of inconstant love in another one:

'These passages and these sentiments are all the right Burns; there is no pallor or insincerity in his feeling for the religion of the cottage, and no half-heartedness in his praise of the life of the road. He who picks and chooses may select from Burns a body of verse to please almost any taste; using it as a text, he may write true and eloquent dissertations on love, on morality, on poetry; but if he refuses to consider the coarse with the fine, the satirical with the devout, the velleities of sentiment with the stark simplicities of passion, he is not writing of Robert Burns.'

There are passages in this prefatory essay when Raleigh (who, as we have seen, considered this to be his very best piece of work) writes even better than he himself estimated, and lets his pen run away with him, with something of the exhilaration of great prose:

'Born as he was into a society of people struggling for a livelihood, and inured to timidities and oppressions, it was only by his enormous gift of courage and candour that he cut himself loose from these bonds, and rose into the freedom of the truth. His magnanimous recklessness speeded him on his way to death, but it was the same quality of his mind which, in the beginning, had lifted him into the light, and delivered him from slavery. He owed a death to the God of whom music and song and blood are pure; he paid his debt early, but he was no loser by the bargain.'

I make no apology for quoting so liberally from this essay which is little known and far from accessible. Its only publication was as a preface to a handsome two-volume edition of J. G. Lockhart's *Life of Robert Burns* which appeared in Liverpool in the fell autumn of the fatal year, 1914, when a twilight had come over the civilised world. (The biography itself was already eighty-six years old, since it came out in 1828.) As Sir Walter Raleigh himself said in a letter:

'No one will ever see it, but it's the best essay on R.B. for all that. It's not *middle-class* like all the other essays.'

In another letter, written in 1921, he said even more truly:

'They both [Henley and Stevenson] treat Burns as if he were the manager of his passions, whereas he well knew that he was the generous victim of them . . . The life of Burns was not long, but it was broad and it was high. He is as proud as Satan (the comparison is his own) and as humble as a child.'

His essay, at its climax, says something final and definitive of all writing about Burns, something to make all his critics feel supererogatory:

'No one was ever franker than Burns. Nothing true can be said of him that has not already been said by himself, somewhere in the six volumes of his collected poems and letters. The whole story of his life is there, so that one cannot but marvel at the multiplication of discussions and disquisitions on his character and career. No matter what the point at issue may be, let the advocates hear it this way and that, the final and convincing word is to be found in his own writings; and seeing that the judge's deliverance was spoken before ever the pleadings began, the topsy-turvy case is likely to be endless . . . Frankness is almost always misconceived. Burns was very like many other men in what he had to tell, and differed from other men only because he told it.'

And the end of Raleigh's essay crowns the work:

'There are few times and seasons when Burns has nothing to say. But he speaks most readily to those who are at the top of happy hours. Lovers meeting at a tryst, soldiers answering the

SCOTT MEETS BURNS IN EDINBURGH

call to action, friends pledging their faith—all these have found in him their Bible. Because he knew happiness he responds to their need. His life is done with; the joy that he took in it remains.' Raleigh, be it noted, was a London-born, Oxford-educated, professor of English at Glasgow University.

Returning to Burns in his own time, Sir Walter Scott's account of his meeting with the poet is to be found in a letter to Lockhart:

'I was a lad of fifteen in 1786–7, when he came first to Edinburgh, but had sense and feeling enough to be much interested in his poetry, and would have given the world to know him; but I had very little acquaintance with any literary people, and still less with the gentry of the west country, the two sets that he most frequented. Mr. Thomas Grierson was at that time a clerk of my father's. He knew Burns, and promised to ask him to his lodgings to dinner, but had no opportunity to keep his word, otherwise I might have seen more of this distinguished man . . .'

That a meeting was subsequently arranged—it happened in the house of Dr. Adam Ferguson—is clear from Scott's passage of direct description in the same letter:

'His person was strong and robust; his manners rustic, not clownish; a sort of dignified plainness and simplicity which received part of its effect perhaps from one's knowledge of his extraordinary talents. His features are represented in Mr. Nasmyth's picture [the familiar best-known portrait] but to me it conveys the idea that they are diminished as if seen in perspective. I think his countenance was more massive than it looks in any of the portraits. I would have taken the poet, had I not known what he was, for a very sagacious country farmer of the old Scotch school—i.e. none of your modern agriculturists, who keep labourers for their drudgery, but the *douce gudeman* who held his own plough. There was a strong expression of sense and shrewdness in all his lineaments; the eye alone, I think, indicated the poetical character and temperament. It was large, and of a dark cast, and glowed (I say literally *glowed*) when he spoke with feeling or interest. I never saw such another eye in a human head, though I have seen the most distinguished men in my time.

'His conversation expressed perfect self-confidence, without the slightest presumption. Among the men who were the most learned of their time and country, he expressed himself with perfect firmness, but without the least intrusive forwardness; and when he differed in opinion, he did not hesitate to express it firmly, yet at the same time with modesty. I do not remember any part of his conversation distinctly enough to be quoted, nor did I ever see him again, except in the street, where he did not recognize me, as I could not expect he should. He was much caressed in Edinburgh, but (considering what literary evolvements have been since his day) the efforts made for his relief were extremely trifling.'

This letter to Lockhart, it should be noted, was written fully forty years after the single conversation between the two great Scots. The house of the encounter was in a street called The Sheens, or Sciennes (which derived its name from its adjacency to the ruins of a monastery dedicated to St. Catherine of Siena). Scott himself described Dr. Ferguson's house as 'a general point of reunion among his friends, particularly of a Sunday, where there generally met, at a hospitable dinner party, the most distinguished literati of the old time who still remained, together with such young persons as were thought worthy to approach their circle and listen to their conversation.'

Another Scot, Robert Buchanan, first-rate journalist and third-rate poet, began his 1891 essay on the subject thus (an essay which my own country will not thank me for quoting):

'Robert Burns was a great man and a great poet, and the influence of his truly tremendous satiric and lyrical genius has been one of the great factors in the disintegration of Scottish superstition . . . He was a convivial creature, and his conviviality was that of a fearless and liberal nature, overflowing with love, and honest as the day. But what was to some extent a virtue in him has become, to my mind, a very curious vice in his disciples. The fact is, Scotchmen seem to have granted Burns his apotheosis chiefly on account of its being an excuse for the consumption of Whisky. So they celebrate this Birthday. So they fill their glasses, hiccup *Auld Lang Syne,* and cry in chorus:

> Robin was a rovin' boy,
>   Rantin' rovin', rantin' rovin';
> Robin was a rovin' boy,
>   Rantin' rovin' Robin.

The drunken squirearchy, whose progenitors broke the poet's heart, and who, if the poet were alive now, would break his heart again, are full of enthusiasm for his memory. Even some of the more liberal-minded ministers of the Gospel join in the acclaim. Farmers and shepherds, factors and ploughmen, all come together on the one great occasion to humour his synonym in the Whisky Bottle. They weep over his woes; they smack their lips over his satire; they shriek at his denunciations, and they murmur his songs. Burns or Bacchus—it is all one. The chief point is that, now or never, there is an excuse for getting "reeling ripe" or "mortal drunk". It is poetic, it is literary, it is—hiccup? —honouring the Muses. Any frenzy, however maniacal, is justifiable under the circumstances. "Glorious Robin!" Pledge him again and again, pledge him and bless him; and when you can't pledge him upright, pledge him prone, as you lie, with your fellow Burns-worshippers, under the table.'

As dog's-abuse this deserves to have its place.

And finally in this nosegay there is the purely English tribute —Sir Leslie Stephen's writing in the *Dictionary of National Biography*:

'Criticism of Burns is only permitted to Scotchmen of pure blood. Admirable appreciations may be found in the essays of Carlyle and Nichol. Yet it may be said that, if there are more elegant and subtle songwriters in the language, no one even approaches Burns in masculine strength or concentrated utterance of passion. Though all his writings are occasional, he reflects every mood of the national character, its tenderness, its sensuous vigour, and its patriotic fervour. Like Byron, he always wrote at a white heat, but, unlike Byron, he had the highest lyrical power, and, if he sometimes fails, he does not fail by excessive dilution. He is only inspired when he tries to adopt the conventional English of his time, in obedience to foolish advice from Dr. Moore and others. The personal character of Burns must be inferred from his life. Its weaker side is well set forth in an essay by Mr. R. L. Stevenson in *The Cornhill* for October, 1879. His coxcombry, however, seems to be there a little exaggerated. Though it may be granted that in his relations to women he showed an unpleasant affectation as well as laxity of morals, it must be said that he was never heartless, that he did his best to support his children, that he was a good father and brother, and that, if his spirit of independence was rather irritable and self-conscious, his pride was, at bottom, thoroughly honourable. In spite of overwhelming difficulties and many weaknesses, and much rash impulsiveness, he struggled hard to "act a manly part" through life. There is less to be forgiven to him than to most of those whose genius has led to morbid developments of character.'

This piece of criticism seems to me to be worth detailed comment and confutation, even though it was written by Sir Leslie Stephen (1832-1904) for the D.N.B. (which that same illustrious man founded). In due course of time Sir Leslie died and his obituary in a supplement of the D.N.B. was duly written by Sir Sidney Lee, who praised his writing for 'a frank sincerity which is vivified by a humorous irony'. If there is none of this humorous irony in Sir Leslie's first sentence, then it is a meaningless first sentence: 'Criticism of Burns is only permitted to Scotchmen of pure blood.'

If Sir Leslie was not here indulging in a canny little joke, what on earth could he mean by this observation? I do not hesitate to ask this question, especially since Sir Leslie Stephen (the father of Virginia Woolf) died in 1905, the year in which I was born. So, who's afraid of Virginia Woolf's father?

WE ARE NA FOU, WE'RE NO THAT FOU,
BUT JUST A DRAPPIE IN OUR EE

7 · *Friends of a Sort*

LET us now revert to some striking and suggestive episodes in the life-history itself. A note, written from Mossgiel in September, 1786, to his friend, the Edinburgh clerk, John Richmond:

'Wish me luck, dear Richmond! Armour has just brought me a fine boy and girl at one throw. God bless the little dears!

> Green grow the rashes, O,
> Green grow the rashes, O,
> A feather bed is no sae saft,
> As the bosoms o' the lasses, O.

Robt. Burns'

Richmond (1765–1846) was born at Sorn in Ayrshire, and Burns first met him when he was a clerk in the lawyer Gavin Hamilton's office at Mauchline. Richmond had a friend of his own age, James Smith, whom he introduced to Burns and who inspired one of the latter's very best verse-epistles. Until Richmond left for Edinburgh at the end of 1785 these three friends were 'unco pack and thick thegither' or, as we might say in English, 'thick as thieves and up to mischief'. They formed the notorious 'Court of Equity' of one of Burns's ribald poems, and they were furthermore all three involved in the frolic which led to the composition of *The Jolly Beggars*. When Burns went to Edinburgh on the publication of his poems he shared a room and a bed with Richmond in Baxter's Close, Lawnmarket. A plaque now marks the building. As the editor of the Letters tells us:

'Their friendship seems to have suffered under the strain of this prolonged intimacy: the poet's few subsequent letters to him are perfunctory in tone.'

This intimacy lasted from November, 1786, until Burns's departure in the following May. In a letter to Richmond in October, 1787, Burns has a notably casual reference to the death of one of his twins:

'By the way I hear I am a girl out of pocket, and by careless murdering mischance, too, which has provoked me and vexed me a good deal.'

Two years later Richmond settled again in Mauchline, and two years after that, in 1791, he married the girl, Jenny Surgeoner, for seducing whom he had had to do public penance in 1785:

'In his later years he declined to talk about Burns, and showed marked impatience when the curious sought to pump him— probably because, like Ainslie and Richard Brown, he did not care to be reminded of the discreditable episodes of his youth.'

James Smith was the recipient of some of Burns's least inhibited letters. From Mauchline on April 28th, 1788, Burns sent him a letter of which this is a flagrant portion:

'There is, you must know, a certain clean-limbed, handsome, bewitching young hussy of your acquaintance, to whom I have lately and privately given a matrimonial title to my corpus. "Bode a robe and wear it," says the wise old Scotch adage! I hate to presage ill luck; and as my girl has been *doubly* kinder to me than even the best of women usually are to their partners of our sex, in similar circumstances, I reckon on twelve times a brace of children against I celebrate my twelfth wedding-day: those twenty-four will give me twenty-four gossippings, twenty-four christenings, (I mean one equal to two), and I hope by the blessing of the God of my fathers, to make them twenty-four dutiful children to their parents, twenty-four useful members of Society, and twenty-four approven servants of their God . . .'

This all-too-proud father proceeds to ask Smith to give him a printed shawl, 'of which I daresay you have variety'—this to be

'my first present to her since I have *irrevocably* called her mine, and I have a kind of whimsical wish to get the said first present from an old and much-valued friend of hers and mine, a trusty trojan, on whose friendship I count myself possessed of a life-rent lease . . .'

Another friend or 'trusty trojan', already mentioned, was Robert Ainslie (1766–1838) to whom Burns wrote about his projected wife in still more jaunty terms. Ainslie hailed from Duns in Berwickshire where his father was Lord Douglas's steward. Burns first met him in 1787 in Edinburgh, where he was a law-student. It was Ainslie who accompanied the poet on the first part of his Border tour in May, that same year, and he paid a visit to the Ellisland farm in October, 1790. The editor of the Letters writes with a well-tempered dryness:

'Ainslie turned pious as he grew older, became an elder in the Kirk, and wrote two small religious works, *A Father's Gift to his Children* and *Reasons for the Hope that is in Us*. His piety, however, did not prevent his preserving, and allowing to be published, the most damaging of his former friend's letters.'

For Ainslie Burns seems to have had even more affection than he had for any other male friend—at this time, at least. In the November of 1787 a letter to Ainslie concludes:

'You will think it romantic when I tell you that I find the idea of your friendship almost necessary to my existence. You assume a proper length of face in my bitter hours of blue-devilism, and you laugh fully up to my highest wishes at my good things.

BOB AINSLIE

I don't know upon the whole, if you are one of the first fellows in God's world, but you are so to me. I tell you this now in the conviction that some inequalities in my temper and manner may perhaps sometimes make you suspect that I am not so warmly as I ought to be—Your friend.'

In January, 1788, he introduced this, 'my dearest friend', to his Clarinda, and he made Ainslie a confidant in his affair with her. It is to the close friendship with Bob Ainslie that we owe two revelations of the very worst side of Burns's nature. One is a letter (sent from Dumfries, 1st June, 1788) asking Ainslie in Edinburgh to visit a servant girl whom Burns had got into trouble and to 'give her ten or twelve shillings', adding the injunction: 'But don't for Heaven's sake meddle with her as a Piece.' This, I am aware, I have already quoted elsewhere. The other is a letter containing an outrageous description of how Burns reunited himself with Jean Armour, who had already borne him twins and who was heavily pregnant with what turned out to be a second pair of twins. Here it is—or at least the relevant passage—in all its deplorable vainglory:

'I have been through sore tribulation and under much buffetting of the Wicked One, since I came to this country. Jean I found banished like a martyr—forlorn, destitute and friendless; all for the good old cause: I have reconciled her to her fate: I have reconciled her to her mother: I have taken her a room: I have taken her to my arms: I have given her a mahogany bed: I have given her a guinea; and I have ———d her till she rejoiced with joy unspeakable and full of glory. But—as I always am on every occasion—I have been provident and cautious to an astounding degree; I swore her, privately and solemnly, never to attempt any claim on me as a husband, even though anyone should persuade her she had such a claim, which she has not, neither during my life, nor after my death. She did all this like a good girl, and I took the opportunity of some dry horselitter, and gave her such a thundering scalade that electrified the very marrow of her bones. O, what a peacemaker is a guid weel-willy pintle! It is the mediator, the guarantee, the umpire, the bond of union, the solemn league and covenant, the plenipotentiary, the Aaron's rod, the Jacob's staff, the prophet Elisha's pot of oil, the Ahaseurus's sceptre, the sword of mercy, the philosopher's stone, the horn of plenty and Tree of Life between Man and Woman.'

This—written on the very day of Jean Armour's second confinement—is an ungainsayable letter. It is seldom quoted, and not at all by the idolaters. But the German authority on Burns, Professor Hans Hecht, denounces the missive as an example of 'downright, elementary, unsurpassable vulgarity', and Hilton Brown, the poet's fairest critic among the moderns, calls it quite simply 'one of the most caddish letters ever penned by mortal man'.

A few days later Burns wrote a quasi-facetious letter on the same subject to his friend Richard Brown:

'I found Jean—with her cargo very well laid in; but unfortunately moor'd, almost at the mercy of wind and tide: I have towed her into harbour where she may lie snug till she unload; and have taken the command myself—not ostensibly, but for a time, in secret—I am gratified by your kind enquiries after her; as after all, I may say with Othello—"Excellent wretch! Perdition catch my soul, but I do love thee!"

Hilton Brown, a not easily shocked commentator, is revolted as much by the brutality as by the swagger of the poet in this episode:

'It throws the most unbearable light on Burns. If he could really commit the act he said he did, in a stable, on a woman over eight months gone with child and showing all the attractions of that physical state, he must have been plain brute. And how much harm did he do his unfortunate twins who were to appear in three weeks, and die in four? But leaving out all the unpleasant implications of the letter, and allowing it to have been written from any ulterior motive open to man, could any human being have written such a letter about a woman he "loved"?'

It should be noted that of the four men-friends with whom this chapter deals, Richmond and Smith and Ainslie were all Burns's juniors by six or seven years, whereas Brown—Captain Richard Brown—was his senior by six years, and had first been met at Irvine where Burns had gone to learn flax-dressing, at the age of twenty-three. Let me recommend a close study of the relationship between these two young men—the sailor twenty-nine and the poet twenty-three when they first met—to those itchy-minded modern writers who cannot bear to imagine that the object of their researches is utterly and unexceptionably heterosexual in his love-life. There is certainly something equivocal about Brown's character. He was a native of the harbour-town of Irvine in North Ayrshire, the son of a simple mechanic and born in 1753. He had received a liberal education paid for by a wealthy patron who took an interest in him. This we know from an eloquent and fervent passage in the long autobiographical letter that Burns sent to Dr. John Moore in 1787 at the request of Mrs. Dunlop, a good friend of both parties. The poet describes his twenty-third year as an important phase in his life:

'But the principal thing which gave my mind a turn was, I formed a bosom-friendship with a young fellow, *the first created being I had ever seen,* [italics mine!] but a hapless son of misfortune. He was the son of a plain mechanic; but a great Man in the neighbourhood taking him under his patronage gave him a genteel education with a view to bettering his station in life.—The Patron dying, just as he was ready to launch forth into the world, the poor fellow in despair went to sea; where after a variety of good and bad fortune, a little before I was acquainted with him, he has been set ashore by an American Privateer on the wild coast of Connaught, stript of everything.—I cannot quit this poor fellow's story without adding that he is at this moment Captain of a large West-Indiaman belonging to the Thames—'

Rob, it is clear, 'lo'ed him like a very brother', and goes on about him:

'This gentleman's mind was fraught with courage, independence, magnanimity, and every noble, manly virtue.—I loved him, I admired him, to a degree of enthusiasm; and I strove to imitate him.—In some measure I succeeded: I had the pride before, but he taught it to flow in proper channels.—His knowledge of the world was vastly superior to mine, and I was all attention to learn.—He was the only man I ever saw who was a greater fool than myself when WOMAN was the presiding star; but he spoke of a certain fashionable failing with levity, which hitherto I had regarded with horror.—Here his friendship did me a mischief . . .'

From Edinburgh in 1787 Burns wrote this remarkable letter to his sailor friend:

'I have met with few things in life which have given me more pleasure than Fortune's kindness to you, since those days when we met in the vale of misery; as I can honestly say, that I never met with a man who more truly deserved it, or to whom my heart more truly wish'd it.—I have been much indebted, since that time, to your story and your sentiments, for steeling my heart against evils of which I have had a pretty decent share.—My will-o'-the-wisp fate you know: do you recollect a Sunday we spent in Eglinton Woods? you told me, on my repeating some verses to you, that you wondered I could resist the temptation of sending verses of such merit to a magazine: 'twas actually this that gave me an idea of my own pieces which encouraged me to endeavour at the character of a Poet.—I am happy to hear that you will be two or three months at home: as soon as a bruised limb will permit me, I shall return to Ayrshire—and we *shall* meet!

> And faith I hope we'll no sit dumb
> Nor yet cast out!

I have much to tell you, "of Men, their manners, and their ways;" and perhaps a little of t'other Sex.—Apropos, I beg to be remembered to Mrs. Brown; there I doubt not, my dear friend, but you have found substantial happiness.—I am impatient to see her, as well as you. I expect to find you something of an altered, but not a different man; the wild, bold, generous young fellow composed into the steady affectionate husband, and the fondly careful Parent.—For me, I am just the same will-o'-the-wisp being I used to be.—About the first, and fourth, quarters of the Moon, I generally set in for the tradewinds of wisdom; but about the full, and change, I am the luckless victim of mad tornadoes, which blow me into chaos.—Almighty Love still "reigns and revels" in my bosom; and I am at this moment ready to hang myself for a young Edinburgh widow, who has wit and beauty more murderously fatal than the assassinating stiletto of the Sicilian banditti, or the poisoned arrow of the savage African. My Highland dirk [he spells it *durk*], that used to hang beside my crutches, I have gravely removed into a neighbouring closet, the key of which I cannot command—in case of spring-tide paroxysms . . .'

And the letter—in which I have sedulously resisted to italicise any particular phrase as being more revealing than any other—concludes with a lyric of Clarinda herself.

But one is unable to forbear quoting a singular paragraph in Sir Compton Mackenzie's book, *On Moral Courage* (published in 1962), all the more so as it follows hard upon that reference to Burns's not very mystical phallicism. He is writing about D. H. Lawrence:

'What must also be understood about Lawrence's mystical phallicism is his discovery that it was a social equaliser. Nobody had less reason to bother about class, but it forever tormented him, and this was why Lady Chatterley had to be the wife of a baronet. It may be significant that many young men who have benefited by the larger opportunities provided by the Welfare State get from Lawrence a reassurance about their own status. When one contrasts Lawrence with Robert Burns, the comparative feebleness of Lawrence is apparent. Burns, who spent much sweeter hours among the lasses than Lawrence ever spent, was never worried about class, and he was able to endow a nation with self-respect without that morbid egopathy which never ceased to trouble Lawrence's spirit. Moreover, Burns had a virility which was denied to Lawrence whose only perfect love affair, according to himself, had been with a young coal-miner.'

In the appendix to his full edition of the Burns Letters, Professor de Lancey Ferguson has an interesting and, of course, highly authoritative note: 'Richard Brown (1753–1833). Brown was born in Irvine, where Burns met him, during the ill-starred venture in flax-dressing . . . After his early misadventures Brown began to prosper. He married and late in 1787 or early 1788 settled in Port Glasgow, which remained his home for the rest of his life. His friendship with Burns ended in a violent quarrel. The poet's charges against his morals had come to his ears, and Brown—like Ainslie, he was settling into smug respectability and desirous of living down the memories of his early wildness— hotly resented them, though his only defence was a counter- charge that Burns was already fully initiated where women were concerned. Almost the only inscribed presentation copy of the Kilmarnock edition which is recorded is the one Burns sent to Brown. After the latter's death it was found hidden away in a sideboard.'

This is a little sad. We shall probably never know by exactly how much Brown broadened Burns's outlook on that unforgotten day long ago in the Eglinton Woods. Or whether the two young men compared notes, or gathered conkers, or brambles, or bluebells, according to the season of the year. Or just read Burns's verses aloud to one another till the sun went down. One might call it, without speculating too far, an afternoon of two fauns instead of one, and leave it at that.

The poet writes from Glasgow to his Clarinda in Edinburgh on the 18th February, 1788, and his letter has the passage:

'I have just met with my old friend, the ship Captain—guess my pleasure—to meet you could alone have given me more . . . I would write you a longer letter but for the present circumstances of my friend.'

To Captain Brown he writes six days later from Mossgiel:

'I arrived here, at my brother's, only yesterday—after fighting my way thro' Paisley and Kilmarnock against those old powerful foes of mine—the Devil, the World, and the Flesh, so terrible in the fields of Dissipation.—I have met with few incidents in my

EGLINTON CASTLE

life which gave me so much pleasure as meeting you in Glasgow. There is a time beyond which we cannot form a tie worth the name of Friendship . . . When I think of life, I resolve to keep a strict look-out in the course of economy, for the sake of worldly convenience and independence of mind; to cultivate intimacy with a few of the companions of Youth, that they may be the friends of Age; never to refuse my liquorish humour a handful of the sweetmeats of life, when they come not too dear; and for Futurity—   The present moment is our aim,
                    The neist we never saw.
How do you like my Philosophy? . . .'

In the following year, 1789, Captain Brown returning from another voyage heard from Burns, now at Ellisland:

'I was just in this country by accident and hearing of your safe arrival, I could not resist the temptation of wishing you joy on your return—wishing you would write me before you sail again —wishing you would always set me down as your bosom-friend— wishing you long life and prosperity and that every good thing may attend you—wishing Mrs. Brown and your little ones as few of the evils of this world as is consistent with humanity—wishing you and she were to make two at the ensuing lying-in with which Mrs. Burns threatens very soon to favour me—wishing that I had longer time to write you at present—and finally wishing that if there is to be another state of existence, Mrs. Brown, Mrs. Burns, our little ones in both families, and you and I in some snug paradisical retreat, may make a jovial party to all Eternity! Amen!!! . . . Farewell! God bless you! my long-loved, dearest friend!!!'

There *have* been cannier Scots than Rabbie in this mood.
    The last surviving letter to the endearing sailor again comes from Ellisland and is dated 4th November, 1789:

'Few things could have given me so much pleasure as the news that you were once more safe and sound on terra firma, and happy in that place where happiness is alone to be found— in the fireside circle . . . No less than an order from the Board of

Excise, at Edinburgh, is necessary before I can have so much time as to meet you in Ayrshire. But do you come, and see me. We must have a social day, and perhaps lengthen it out with half the night, before you go again to sea. You are the earliest friend I now have on earth, my brothers excepted; and is not that an endearing circumstance? When you and I first met, we were at the green period of human life. The twig would easily take a bent, but would as easily return to its former state. You and I not only took a bent, but by the melancholy, though strong, influence of being both of the family of the unfortunate, we were entwined with one another in our growth towards advanced age; and blasted be the sacrilegious hand that shall attempt to undo the union! You and I must have one bumper to my favourite toast, "May the companions of your youth be the friends of our old age!" Come and see me one year; I shall see you at Port-Glasgow the next: and if we can contrive to have a gossiping between our two bedfellows, it will be so much additional pleasure. Mrs. Burns joins me in kind compliments to you and Mrs. Brown. Adieu!'

Let me, finally, pass on my scandalous suggestion about Burns and Brown to any non-idolator who cares to follow it up and to speculate further. Incidentally, a tablet was erected in the woods near Irvine by the Irvine Burns Club in 1927. It reads exactly as follows:

THE DRUKKEN STEPS (ST. BRYDE'S WELL)—EGLINTON WOODS

Favourite Walk, 1781–82, of Robert Burns and his sailor friend, Richard Brown.

"Do you recollect a Sunday we spent together in Eglinton Woods?"   *(Edinburgh, 30th December, 1787)*

ALLOWAY'S AULD HAUNTED KIRK

8 · Tam, Ah Tam!

THE fundamental idea of *Tam o' Shanter* we owe to the most extraordinary and remarkable of all of Burns's friends, the antiquary called Francis Grose who was born in the village of Greenford in Middlesex (which is now merely a part of Greater London). But he had romantic origins and attributes. He was the son of a rich Swiss jeweller who had settled in Richmond. Between the ages of twenty-four and thirty-two he studied antiques and heraldry at the Herald's College, and then became adjutant of the Hampshire and Surrey militia. When his easy and extravagant habits had cost him the fortune he had inherited, he decided to profit from the studies of his youth, and from his draughtsmanship at which he was adept. He published his illustrated books, *Antiquities of England and Wales*, between the years 1773 and 1787 and they proved very successful. With the idea of writing a sequel, Captain Grose set out on an antiquarian tour through Scotland in 1789. His rich humour and good nature and his splendid social qualities made him friends everywhere, including Burns, whom he met at Friar's Carse in Nithsdale. The poet has left a description in a letter to Mrs. Dunlop which is dated 17th July, 1789, and was sent from Ellisland:

'Captain Grose, the well-known Author of the Antiquities of England and Wales, has been through Annandale, Nithsdale and Galloway, in the view of commencing another Publication, The Antiquities of Scotland.—As he has made his headquarters with Captain Riddell, my nearest neighbour, for these two months, I am intimately acquainted with him; and I have never seen a man of more original observation, anecdote and remark. —Thrown into the army from the Nursery, and now that he is the father of a numerous family who are all settled in respectable situations in life, he has mingled in all societies and known everybody.—His delight is to steal thro' the country almost unknown, both as most favourable to his humor and his business. —I have to the best of my recollection of the old buildings etc. in the County, given him an Itinerary thro' Ayrshire.—I have directed him among other places to Dunlop House, as an old building worthy of a place in his Collection.—It would have been presumption in such a man as I, to offer an introductory letter between such folks as Captain Grose and Major Dunlop, tho' for the honour of my native county I could have wished that Captain Grose had been introduced to the Dunlop family, and the Major would have been much use to him in directing him thro' the farther corner of Cunningham, a place I little know, however if you discover a cheerful-looking grig of an old fat fellow, the precise figure of Dr. Slop, wheeling about your avenue in his own carriage with a pencil and paper in his hand, you may conclude, "Thou art the man!"—Perhaps after all I may pluck up as much impudent importance as write to the Major by him.—He will go for Ayrshire [a slip, obviously, for *Cunningham*] in four or five days, but I have directed him thro' Carrick and Kyle first.—'

Non-Ayrshire readers must perhaps be informed that Ayrshire was—and still is—divided into three sections or provinces: Cunningham in the north, with Kilmarnock its capital town; Kyle in the middle with Ayr as its chief town; and Carrick in the south with Maybole as its ancient capital.

Burns took to this jovial man, and his reference to a character in *Tristram Shandy* makes us envisage the antiquarian—apparently Grose in name and gross in nature—as an illustration to Laurence Sterne by Thomas Rowlandson. The poet had suggested the ruined Kirk at Alloway as a subject for the new book of Scottish antiquities. We have the reliable word of the poet's brother, Gilbert, that Grose agreed, on condition that Robert provided a legend of witches to go with the drawing. In June, 1790, Burns provided Grose with a witch-tale in prose, and followed it up with the masterly version in verse which is, quite simply, the most exciting narrative poem since Chaucer. Grose naturally preferred the poem to the prose narration, and published it in his *Antiquities of Scotland* of April, 1791, though it had already appeared in the *Edinburgh Magazine* in the previous month. The prose version is interesting and little known, and should occasionally be transcribed in the hope that it may incite lazy southerners to read *Tam o' Shanter* itself with the aid of a glossary. Here it is:

'On a market day, in the town of Ayr, a farmer from Carrick, and consequently whose way lay by the very gate of Alloway Kirk-yard, in order to cross the river Doon at the old bridge, which is about two or three hundred yards farther on than the said gate, had been detained by his business, till by the time he reached Alloway it was the wizard hour between night and morning.

'Though he was terrified by a blaze streaming from the Kirk, yet as it is a well known fact, that to turn back on these occasions is running by far the greatest risk of mischief, he prudently advanced on his road. When he had reached the gate of the Kirk-yard, he was surprised and entertained, through the ribs and arches of an old Gothic window, which still faces the highway, to see a dance of witches merrily footing it round their old sooty blackguard master, who was keeping all alive with the power of his bagpipe. The farmer, stopping his horse to observe them a little, could plainly descry the faces of many old women of his acquaintance and neighbourhood. How the gentleman (i.e. the Prince of Darkness) was dressed, tradition does not say, but that the ladies were all in their smocks; and one of them happening unluckily to have a smock which was considerably too short to answer all the purposes of that piece of dress, our farmer was so tickled that he involuntarily burst out, with a loud laugh, "Weel looppen Maggy wi' the short sark!" and, recollecting himself, instantly spurred his horse to the top of his speed. I need not mention the universally known fact, that no diabolical power can pursue you beyond the middle of a running stream. Lucky it was for the poor farmer that the river Doon was so near, for notwithstanding the speed of his horse, which was a good one, against he reached the middle of the arch of the bridge, and

BY SOME AULD HOULET-HAUNTED BIGGIN,
OR KIRK DESERTED BY HER RIGGIN'

consequently the middle of the stream, the pursuing, vengeful hags were so close at his heels, that one of them actually sprang to seize him; but it was too late; nothing was on her side of the stream but the horse's tail, which immediately gave way at her infernal grip, as if blasted by a stroke of lightning; but the farmer was beyond her reach. However, the unsightly, tailless condition of the vigorous steed was, to the last hours of the noble creature's life, an awful warning to the Carrick farmers not to stay too late in Ayr markets.'

It is curious to note that in this sketch of the marvellous yarn there is no mention of the thunderstorm through which Tam rode, which roars and clatters in the poem from start to finish, and which is one of the best-described tempests in the whole of literature, prose or verse. It may be noted, too, that the horse of the prose becomes a mare (in Ayrshire, then as now, pronounced *meer*)* in the poem, and that her name Maggy is oddly enough given to the witch Cutty Sark in the prose version.

Curiouser still is the fact that there is a Galloway legend of the witch story, with important differences from the Ayrshire one on which Burns based his poem. The biographer Lockhart says of *Tam o' Shanter*:

'The admirable execution of the piece, so far as it goes, leaves nothing to wish for; the only criticism has been that the catastrophe appears unworthy of the preparation.'

Tam escapes scot-free and did not apparently lose even so much as his tam-o'-shanter bonnet. It is only the poor mare Meg or Maggy who loses anything—her tail—as a result of her master's drunken impulse. In the Galloway version poor Maggie loses her life as well as her tail.

But Lockhart is worth scrutiny on the point:

'Burns might have avoided this error,—if error it be,—had he followed not the Ayrshire, but the Galloway, edition of the legend. According to that tradition, the *Cutty Sark* who attracted the special notice of the bold intruder on the Satanic ceremonial, was no other than the pretty wife of a farmer residing in the same village with himself, and of whose unholy propensities no sus-

* For confirmation of this fact see the last line of the quoted passage in Burns's own hand.

picion had ever been whispered. The Galloway *Tam* being thoroughly sobered by terror, crept to his bed the moment he reached home after his escapade, and said nothing of what had happened to any of his family. He was awakened in the morning with the astounding intelligence that his horse had been found dead in the stable, and a woman's hand, clotted with blood, adhering to the tail. Presently it was reported that Cutty Sark had burnt her hand grievously over-night, and was ill in bed, but obstinately refused to let her wound be examined by the village leech. Hereupon Tam, disentangling the bloody hand from the hair of his defunct favourite's tail, proceeded to the residence of the fair witch, and forcibly pulling her stump to view, showed his trophy, and narrated the whole circumstances of the adventure. The poor victim of the black-art was constrained to confess her guilty practices in presence of the priest and the laird, and was forthwith burnt alive, under their joint auspices, within watermark on the Solway Firth.'

This is the version which was current up to a century ago in Galloway—a district or region which takes in the whole of Kirkcudbright and parts of Wigtown, Dumfriesshire, and South Ayrshire. On the whole Burns chose wisely to adhere to the mid-Ayrshire version as he had heard it in his youth. It is perhaps better for artistic propriety that the mare should lose her tail than that the witch should lose her hand. But the variant is at least interesting and should be better known.

Grose's best memorial is Burns's jolly and rumbustious poem entitled *On the Late Captain Grose's Peregrinations thro' Scotland, Collecting Antiquities of that Kingdom.* This first appeared in an Edinburgh newspaper, the *Evening Courant,* in 1789, and was later included in the 1793 edition of Burns's poems. Meanwhile Grose had died in Dublin in 1791, of an apoplexy.

> Hear, Land o' Cakes, and brither Scots,
> Frae Maidenkirk to Johnny Groats;—
> If there's a hole in a' your coats,
>   I rede you tent it:
> A chiel's amang you taking notes,
>   And, faith, he'll prent it . . .

But since the non-Scottish reader will already be in difficulties by the fourth line, let me give the whole poem in William Kean Seymour's anglicised version (fully aware that the volume called *Burns into English* by this ingenious 'translator', first published in 1954, is anathematised by Burns-worshippers):

> Hear, Land of Cakes, and brother Scots
> From Maidenkirk to Johnny Groats;—
> If there's a hole in all your coats
>   I beg you'll mend it:
> A lad's among you taking notes,
>   And, faith, he'll print it.
>
> If in your bounds ye chance to light
> Upon a person plump and tight,
> Of stature short, but genius bright,
>   That's he, the joker!
> And my! he has uncommon sleight
>   With chalk and ochre.
>
> By some owl-haunted ancient building
> Or church without a roof for shielding,
> It's ten to one you'll find him sealed in
>   Some spectral part,
> With devils—save our souls!—colleaguing
>   In some black art.
>
> Each ghost that haunts old hall or chamber,
> Ye gipsy gang that deal in glamour,
> And you, deep read in Hell's black grammar,
>   Warlocks and witches—
> Ye'll quake to hear his magic hammer,
>   Ye midnight bitches!
>
> It's told he was a soldier bred,
> Who would have rather fall'n than fled;
> But now he's quit the gallant blade
>   And dog-skin wallet,
> And joined the—Antiquarian trade,
>   I think they call it.

He has a store of old knicknackets,
Rusty iron caps and jingling jackets,
Would keep the Lothians three in tackets
    A twelvemonth good;
And porridge-pots and old salt-buckets
    Before the Flood.

Of Eve's first fire he has a cinder;
Old Tubal Cain's fire-scoop and fender;
That which distinguished clear the gender
    Of Balaam's ass;
A broom-stick of the Witch of Endor,
    Well-shod with brass.

Besides, he'll shape you on his leg
The cut of Adam's filibeg;
The knife that snickered Abel's crag—
    He'll prove you fully
It was a folding pocket rig
    Or long-kale gully.

But would ye see him in his glee,
For generous glee and fun has he,
Then set him down, with two or three
    Good fellows by him;
And port, O port! shine thou a wee,
    And then ye'll spy him!

Now, by the Powers of verse and prose,
Thou art a worthy lad, O Grose!
Whoe'er of thee shall ill suppose,
    They sore miscall thee;
I'd take the rascal by the nose,
    With 'Shame befall thee!'

I suggest, with quite as much respect to Mr. Kean Seymour as to Burns, that this is the text clarified if not improved. Compare the second stanza with that of the original—the new version of the last three lines has wit as well as ingenuity. This is the Burns:

If in your bounds ye chance to light
Upon a fine, fat, fodgel wight,
O' stature short, but genius bright,
   That's he, mark weel!
And wow! he has an unco sleight
   O' cauk and keel.

I would only say here that there is much less to be said for modernisation in the case of the serious poems and lyrics than in that of the light and jaunty verse, of which these particular lines offer so good an example. Willingly and readily I agree that a little masterpiece of a song like *Ca' the Yowes* cannot be 'translated' without being gravely damaged and spoiled. The song begins:

Ca' the yowes to the knowes,
Ca' them where the heather grows,
Ca' them where the burnie rows,
   My bonnie dearie.

Hark! the mavis' evening sang
Sounding Clouden's woods amang;
Then a-faulding let us gang,
   My bonnie dearie . . .

And the Kean Seymour version begins unacceptably like this:

Call the ewes to the knolls,
Call them mid the heather bells,
Call them where the wild brook rolls,
   My bonnie dearie.

Hark! the thrush's evening song
Sounding Clouden's woods amang;
Then a-folding let's along,
   My bonnie dearie . . .

This winna dae! Burns, once one has learned to pierce his dialect, is at heart a simple poet, seldom profound. This is why he has been translated into many languages, and it is his simplicity as well as his socialism which appealed to the Soviet poet, Samuel Marshak, whose translations have made Burns today almost the most popular of all British poets in the U.S.S.R. He has, in fact, been successfully translated into most European languages—excepting English!

If I wanted to give any English godchild of mine a taste for Burns I should ask him to memorise—not a masterpiece like *Tam o' Shanter*, which for all its genius is full of off-putting Scotch, nor yet the famous lines to the mouse or the daisy which are fundamentally sentimental, for all their fame. No, I should submit some lesser-known but quite perfect thing like the *Epistle to a Young Friend* which was written in May of the year 1786, the year of the Kilmarnock edition of his poems. The identity of the young friend is unknown—we only know his first name to be Andrew. This is the poem I should first submit to the godchild— or to the non-Scottish lover of poetry—for many reasons. And since the modern reader tends to skip any poem of any length, let me submit it to him two stanzas—or two spoonfuls—at a time. The verse strikes the right happy medium between the thick Scottish vernacular and the stilted and formal English style which did not suit Burns in the least:

I lang hae thought, my youthfu' friend,
 A something to have sent you,
Tho' it should serve nae ither end
 Than just a kind memento:
But how the subject-theme may gang,
 Let time and chance determine:
Perhaps it may turn out a sang,
 Perhaps, turn out a sermon.

Ye'll try the world soon, my lad;
 And, Andrew dear, believe me,
Ye'll find mankind an unco squad,
 And muckle they may grieve ye:
For care and trouble set your thought,
 Even when your end's attainèd;
And a' your views may come to nought,
 Where ev'ry nerve is strainèd.

The only glossarising so far really necessary is that 'unco' when used—as here—as an adjective signifies 'strange' or 'uncouth', whereas when used—as more usually in Burns—adverbially, as it is in the next verse, it simply means 'very' (short for 'uncommonly', as it were):

> I'll no say men are villains a':
>   The real harden'd wicked,
> Wha hae nae check but human law,
>   Are to a few restrickèd;
> But och! mankind are unco weak,
>   An' little to be trusted;
> If *self* the wavering balance shake,
>   It's rarely right adjusted!
>
> Yet they wha fa' in Fortune's strife,
>   Their fate we shouldna censure;
> For still th' important end of life
>   They equally may answer:
> A man may hae an honest heart,
>   Tho' poortith hourly starè him,
> A man may tak a neebor's part,
>   Yet hae nae cash to spare him.

No great English discernment is called for, surely, to perceive that restrickèd' is 'restricted' and that 'poortith' is 'poverty'?

> Ay free, aff han', your story tell,
>   When wi' a bosom cronie;
> But still keep something to yoursel
>   Ye scarcely tell to onie:
> Conceal yourself as weel's ye can
>   Frae critical dissection:
> But keek thro' ev'ry other man,
>   Wi' sharpen'd, sly inspection.
>
> The sacred lowe o' weel-plac'd love,
>   Luxuriantly indulge it;
> But never tempt th'illicit rove,
>   Tho' naething should divulge it:

I waive the quantum o' the sin,
   The hazard of concealing;
But och! it hardens a' within,
   And petrifies the feeling!

'Lowe'—pronounced to rhyme with 'now'—is a beautiful old
Scottish word (still in use) for 'fire' or 'blaze' or 'flame'.

To catch Dame Fortune's golden smile,
   Assiduous wait upon her;
And gather gear by ev'ry wile
   That's justified by honour!
Not for to hide it in a hedge,
   Nor for a train attendant;
But for the glorious privilege
   Of being independent.

The fear o' Hell's a hangman's whip
   To haud the wretch in order;
But where ye feel your honour grip,
   Let that ay be your border:
Its slightest touches, instant pause—
   Debar a' side-pretences;
And resolutely keep its laws,
   Uncaring consequences.

And all that needs explaining in the last three stanzas is that
'ranting' in Burns means not so much 'raving' or 'talking wildly'
as 'noisy, full of animal spirits'.

The great Creator to revere,
   Must sure become the creature;
But still the preaching cant forbear
   And ev'n the rigid feature:
Yet ne'er with wits profane to range
   Be complaisance extended;
An atheist-laugh's a poor exchange
   For Deity offended.

When ranting round in Pleasure's ring,
    Religion may be blinded;
Or if she gie a random sting,
    It may be little minded;
But when on Life we're tempest-driv'n—
    A conscience but a canker—
A correspondence fix'd wi' Heav'n,
    Is sure a noble anchor.

Adieu, dear amiable youth!
    Your heart can ne'er be wanting!
May prudence, fortitude, and truth,
    Erect your brow undaunting!
In ploughman phrase, 'God send you speed',
    Still daily to grow wiser;
And may ye better reck the rede
    Than ever did th'adviser!

'Reck the rede' is 'heed the advice', and is Old English and not Scottish, and it irresistibly reminds us of what Ophelia said to her brother Laertes when acknowledging his highly moral counsel and bidding him goodbye:

I shall the effect of this good lesson keep
As watchman to my heart; but, good my brother,
Do not as some ungracious pastors do,
Show me the steep and thorny way to heaven,
Whiles like a puff'd and reckless libertine,
Himself the primrose path of dalliance treads,
And recks not his own rede.

This is precisely how the unknown Andrew might have acknowledged this *Epistle to a Young Friend* if he had had the wit. And Burns himself in his delightful last stanza obviously had the wit to envisage the possibility.

Two Burnsian references from major novelists may here provide an appropriate interlude. The first is Dickens, who has an indirect reference by one of his greatest characters in one of the greatest novels. But before this one must express sad disappointment at finding no song of Burns in the varied repertoire with which that amateur vocalist Dick Swiveller regaled the club of his own founding, the Glorious Apollers. The character who does quote Burns, though without mentioning him by name, is Wilkins Micawber himself. He pauses perplexedly at the word 'gowans', apparently unaware that this means no more and no less than 'daisies', and even Copperfield cannot enlighten him, which is very English of both of them. It is in the twenty-eighth chapter:

'"Punch, my dear Copperfield," said Mr. Micawber, tasting it, "like time and tide, waits for no man. Ah! it is at the present moment in high flavour. My love, will you give me your opinion?"'

'Mrs. Micawber pronounced it excellent.

'"Then I will drink," said Mr. Micawber, "if my friend Copperfield will permit me to take that social liberty, to the days when my friend Copperfield and myself were younger, and fought our way in the world side by side. I may say, of myself and Copperfield, in words we have sung together before now, that

'We twa hae run about the braes
An pu'd the gowans fine'
—in a figurative point of view—on several occasions. I am not exactly aware," said Mr. Micawber, with the old roll in his voice, and the old indescribable air of saying something genteel, "what gowans may be, but I have no doubt that Copperfield and myself would frequently have taken a pull at them, if it had been feasible."

'Mr. Micawber, at the then present moment, took a pull at his punch. So we all did: Traddles evidently lost in wondering at what distant time Mr. Macawber and I could have been comrades in the battle of the novelist.'

The second great novelist, and one with a far more extended and direct reference to the poet is Jane Austen in her maddeningly short fragment of a novel called *Sanditon*. In this scene the heroine Charlotte Heywood is quizzed by the intellectual fop, Sir Edward Denham:

' "But while we are on the subject of poetry, what think you, Miss Heywood, of Burns's lines to his Mary? Oh! there is pathos to madden one! If ever there was a man who *felt*, it was Burns. Montgomery has all the fire of poetry, Wordsworth has the true soul of it, Campbell has touched the extreme of our sensations— 'Like angels' visits, few and far between! Can you conceive any thing more subduing, more melting, more fraught with the deep sublime than that line? But Burns—I confess my sense of his pre-eminence, Miss Heywood. If Scott *has* a fault, it is the want of passion. Tender, elegant, descriptive—but *tame*. The man who cannot do justice to the attributes of women is my contempt. Sometimes indeed a flash of feeling seems to irradiate him, as in the lines we were speaking of—'Oh! Woman in our hours of ease'. But Burns is always on fire. His soul was the altar in which lovely woman sat enshrined, his spirit truly breathed the immortal incense which is her due." '

Charlotte, as soon as she had the opportunity, interrupted this flow of words and sentiment, with the observation:

' "I have read several of Burns's poems with great delight, but I am not poetic enough to separate a man's poetry entirely from his character; and poor Burns's known irregularities greatly interrupt my enjoyment of his lines. I have difficulty in depending on the truth of his feelings as a lover. I have not faith in the *sincerity* of the affections of a man of his description. He felt and he wrote and he forgot." '

This last loaded little sentence drove Sir Edward into what Miss Austen called an ecstasy of protest:

' "Oh! no, no, he was all ardour and truth! His genius and his susceptibilities might lead him into some aberrations. But who is perfect? It were hypercriticism, it were pseudo-philosophy to expect from the soul of high-toned genius, the grovelling of a common mind. The coruscations of talent, elicited by impassioned feeling in the breast of man, are perhaps incompatible with some of the prosaic decencies of life; nor can you, loveliest Miss Heywood, (with an air of deep sentiment), nor can any woman be a fair judge of what a man may be propelled to say, write or do, by the sovereign impulses of illimitable ardour."'

This was very fine, comments Miss Austen—but, if Charlotte understood it all, not very *moral*, and being by no means pleased with his extraordinary style of compliment, she gravely answered:

'"I really know nothing of the matter. This is a charming day. The wind I fancy must be southerly."'

The change of topic was quite ineffectual since the egregious young man replied:

' "Happy, happy wind, to engage Miss Heywood's thoughts!" '

And Miss Austen finally comments:

'She began to think him downright silly. His choosing to walk with her she had learnt to understand. It was done to pique Miss Brereton. She had read it, in an anxious glance or two on his side, but why he should talk so much nonsense, unless he could do no better, was unintelligible. He seemed very sentimental, very full of some feelings or other, and very much addicted to all the newest fashioned hard words, had not a very clear brain she presumed, and talked a good deal by rote.'

Poor Burns's known irregularities? It is a wonderful conjecture—how much did Miss Austen know of them?

THE PRIEST-LIKE FATHER READS THE SACRED PAGE

9 · *Reversion to Criticism*

THERE is a relevant passage in the *Table Talk* of the incomparable
Hazlitt, whom it never does to neglect on *any* subject:

'The public now are the posterity of Milton and Shakespeare.
Our posterity will be the living public of a future generation.
When a man is dead, they put money in his coffin, erect monu-
ments to his memory, and celebrate the anniversary of his
birthday in set speeches. Would they take any notice of him if
he were living? No!—I was complaining of this to a Scotchman
who had been attending a dinner and a subscription to raise a
monument to Burns. He replied, he would sooner subscribe
twenty pounds to his monument than have given him it while
living; so that if the poet were to come to life again, he would
treat him just as he was treated in fact. This was an honest
Scotchman. What *he* said, the rest would do.'

The clear implication is that Hazlitt's view of the average
Scot—like Dr. Johnson's and Charles Lamb's—was, to put it

mildly, unfavourable. It is no less clear that in his view 'an honest Scotchman' was the exception rather than the rule. Those who are not Scottish—that is, those who are too impartial to be indignant on the subject—should hunt out a rarity in Hazlitt's writings where he expresses his view of the Scottish character in blistering fashion. It is an essay called *On the Scotch Character* which appeared in 1822 in *The Liberal*. It was first republished in 1904 in the volume of *Fugitive Writings* in the collected works (edited by Waller and Glover). It begins: 'The Scotch nation are a body-corporate. They hang together like a swarm of bees.' It continues: 'If you see a Scotchman in the street, you may be almost sure it is another Scotchman he is in arm in arm with; and what is more, you may be sure they are talking of Scotchmen.' This is just a shade exaggerated—they are sometimes talking of Scotland itself.

It continues in this vein for two thousand words—all very caustic, subtle, severe, and called-for. And it concludes:

'A Scotchman acts always from a motive, and on due consideration; and if he does not act right or with a view to honest ends, is more dangerous than any one else. Others may plead the vices of their blood in extenuation of their errors; but a Scotchman is a machine, and should be constructed on sound moral and philosophical principles, or should be put a stop to altogether.'

All this points in the direction of that observation of my own, that whereas the Scotsman loudly declares himself *ad nauseam* to be the Lord of Creation, the Englishman smilingly and silently *knows* he is.

But Hazlitt on Burns—whom he clearly regards as one of those exceptionally honest Scots—is altogether less grating and more affable. His note on Burns in an anthology he made in 1824, *Select British Poets,* must placate even the idolatrous:

'One might be tempted to write an elegy rather than a criticism on him. In naivety, in spirit, in characteristic humour, in vivid description of natural objects and of the natural feelings of the heart, he has left behind him no superior.'

But the Scotophobic Hazlitt's appreciation of his Scots poet is most in evidence in the seventh of his *Lectures on the English Poets* which were delivered at the Surrey Institution in the year 1818, and published in the same year. This particular lecture is entitled *On Burns, and the Old English Ballads*. It is eloquent, highly characteristic in its allusiveness, and could not be more appreciative if Hazlitt had Scots blood in him—of which he had no jot or tittle:

'Shakespeare says of some one, that "he was like a man made after supper of a cheese-paring". Burns, the poet, was not such a man. He had a strong mind, and a strong body, the fellow to it. He had a real heart of flesh and blood beating in his bosom— you can almost hear it throb. Someone said, that if you had shaken hands with him, his hand would have burnt yours. The Gods, indeed, "made him poetical"; but Nature had a hand in him first. His heart was in the right place. He did not "create a soul under the ribs of death", by tinkling siren sounds, or by piling up centos of poetic diction; but for the artificial flowers of poetry, he plucked the mountain-daisy under his feet; and a field-mouse, hurrying from its ruined dwelling, could inspire him with the sentiments of terror and pity . . .'

Then the true critic begins to take over from the unusual eulogist:

'Burns was not like Shakespeare in the range of genius; but there is something of the same magnanimity, directness, and unaffected character about him. He was not a sickly senti-mentalist, a namby-pamby poet, a mincing metre ballad-monger, any more than Shakespeare . . . He was as much of a man—not a twentieth part as much of a poet as Shakespeare. With but little of his imagination or inventive power, he had the same life of mind: within the narrow circle of personal feeling or domestic incidents, the pulse of his poetry flows as healthily and vigorously. He had an eye to see; a heart to feel; no more. His pictures of good fellowship, of social glee, of quaint humour, are equal to anything; they come up to nature, and they cannot

WILLIAM HAZLITT

go beyond it. The sly jest collected in his laughing eye at the sight of the grotesque and ludicrous in manners—the large tear rolled down his manly cheek at the sight of another's distress. He has made us as well acquainted with himself as it is possible to be; has let out the honest impulses of his native disposition, the unequal conflict of the passions in his breast, with the same frankness and truth of description. His strength is not greater than his weakness: his virtues were greater than his vices. His virtues belonged to his genius: his vices to his situation, which did not correspond to his genius.'

When Hazlitt in his lecture arrived at the masterly *Tam o' Shanter* he said: 'I shall give the beginning of it, but I am afraid that I shall hardly know when to leave off.' It is pleasant to find the whole poem quoted, so we must assume that the lecturer did *not* leave off. And at the end he has the comment:

'Burns has given the extremes of licentious eccentricity and convivial enjoyment, in the story of this scapegrace, and of patriarchal simplicity and gravity in describing the old national character of the Scottish peasantry.'

It is only on the subject of *The Cotter's Saturday Night* that I am out of accord with this great critic's appreciation of Burns. I have since my earliest Burns-soaked days had the conviction that Burns wrote this poem with his tongue in his cheek. A cotter is a farmworker inhabiting a cottage or 'cote-house' of his own, and a cotter, in Burns's time even more than today, spent his Saturday night in the taverns of the nearest town or village, and as often as not went home at midnight roaring, or at least singing, drunk. With the morning and its headaches, penitence set in. And I should be altogether more disposed to take Burns's eclogue seriously if he had called it *The Cotter's Sabbath Night*. However, this is an idiosyncratic view. Here is my revered Hazlitt on the subject:

'*The Cotter's Saturday Night* is a noble and pathetic picture of human manners, mingled with a fine religious awe. It comes over the mind like a slow and solemn strain of music. The soul of the poet aspires from this scene of low-thoughted care, and reposes, in trembling hope, on "the bosom of its Father and its God".'

Well may Hazlitt quote—or misquote, as his curious custom was—the last line of Thomas Gray's famous *Elegy*. The eight stanzas of the Burns poem which he proceeded to quote are a wordy paraphrase of what Gray had the art to put into a dozen lines.

Another and even more detached and objective professor— the Cornishman, Sir Arthur Quiller-Couch—is again a powerful advocate in Burns's favour. In a lecture on Dorothy Wordsworth he says of the Scottish poet in a significant parenthesis: 'Burns— whom I worship, and, I really do think, a little more intelligently than the mass of his countrymen . . .' And he had another amusing reference to bardolatry in a speech he made to the Edinburgh Sir Walter Scott Club in 1926:

SIR ARTHUR QUILLER-COUCH

'Many years ago I found myself in very hot water through asking innocently in a weekly paper why Scotsmen spent such a disproportionate amount of enthusiasm on Burns as compared with Scott. I shall not revive that controversy to-night, for fear of physical violence, save to say that had I the honour to be one of Scott's countrymen I would beat the racial tom-tom in his honour above all other men of your jealous race.'

Reasonably à propos is one of Charles Lamb's many flying references to Burns in his Letters:

'You remind me of a Scotchman who assured me that he did not see much in Shakespeare. I replied, I dare say *not*. He felt the equivoque, looked awkward, and reddish, but soon returned to the attack, by saying that he thought Burns was as good as Shakespeare: I said that I had no doubt he was—to a *Scotchman*. We exchanged no more words that day.'

Another famous letter-writer, Edward FitzGerald, also has his more or less teasing comments. He compares Burns not with Shakespeare but with Béranger. The comparison is raised in one of his letters to Fanny Kemble who had already made it herself:

'What inspires me now is that, about the time you were writing to me about Burns and Béranger, I was thinking of them "which was the Greater Genius?"—I can't say; but, with all my Admiration for about a Score of the Frenchman's almost perfect Songs, I would give all of them up for a Score of Burns' Couplets, Stanzas, or single Lines scattered among those quite *im*perfect Lyrics of his. Béranger, no doubt, was the *Artist,* which still is not the highest Genius—witness Shakespeare, Dante, Aeschylus, Calderon, to the contrary. Burns assuredly had more *Passion* than the Frenchman; which is not *Genius* either, but a great Part of the Lyric Poet still. What Béranger might have been, if born and bred among Banks, Braes, and Mountains, I cannot tell: Burns has that advantage over him. And then the Highland Mary to love, amid the heather, as compared to Lise the Grisette in a Parisian Suburb! Some of the old French virelays and *Vaux-de-vire* come much nearer the Wild Notes of Burns, and go to one's heart like his; Béranger never gets so far as that, I think. One knows he will come round to his pretty *refrain* with perfect grace; if he were more Inspired he couldn't.

> My Love is like the red, red Rose
> That's newly sprung in June,
> My Love is like the Melody
> That's sweetly play'd in tune—

and he will love his Love, "Till a' the Seas gang dry." Yes—

"till a' the Seas gang dry, my Dear." And then comes some weaker stuff about Rocks melting in the Sun. All imperfect— but that Red, Red Rose has burned itself into one's silly Soul in spite of all.'

And the editor of these letters has a significant footnote: 'There are things that Béranger could not reach with all his art: but Burns could without it.'

FitzGerald's great friend Tennyson also thought highly of Burns's poetry, especially of his songs; and wrote in 1848 to his friend Aubrey de Vere after a tour in Scotland:

'On the whole perhaps I enjoyed no day more than the one I spent at Kirk Alloway by the monument of poor Burns, and the orchards, and "banks and braes of bonny Doon". I made a pilgrimage thither out of love for the great peasant; they were gathering in the wheat, and the spirit of the man mingled, or seemed to mingle, with all I saw. I know you do not care much for him, but I do, and hold that there never was immortal poet if he be not one.'

Alfred Tennyson described this pilgrimage in another letter to FitzGerald, declaring that it moved him to 'a passion of tears'. And FitzGerald quoting this to Fanny Kemble has the dry comment: 'And A.T. not given to the melting mood at all!'

Hallam Tennyson in his memoir of his father gives a neat little exchange of contrary opinions:

'Not less ardent was his enthusiasm for Burns. And here an incident with no small significance returns to me. "Read the exquisite songs of Burns," he exclaimed. "In shape, each of them has the perfection of the berry; in light the radiance of the dewdrop; you forget for its sake those stupid things, his serious pieces!" The same day I met Wordsworth, and named Burns to him. Wordsworth praised him, even more vehemently than Tennyson had done, as the great genius who had brought Poetry back to Nature; but ended, "Of course I refer to his serious efforts, such as the *Cotter's Saturday Night;* those foolish little amatory songs of his one has to forget." I told the tale to

ALFRED, LORD TENNYSON

Henry Taylor that evening; and his answer was: "Burns' exquisite songs and Burns' serious efforts are to me alike tedious, and disagreeable reading!" So much for the infallibility of Poets in their own art!'

In one of his causeries in *John o' London's Weekly*, in the ghastly dark year of 1943, Robert Lynd had a lightly agreeable enquiry entitled *Burns the Universal Brother* which was not, I think, ever reprinted:

'How many of you, I wonder—those of you, at least, who were born outside Scotland—read Burns nowadays? Southern critics have, in recent years, paid little attention to him. I have met

Englishmen [Lynd himself was Northern Irish] who said that the language he wrote is too difficult for them. They affirmed that, little Latin though they learnt at school, they could translate Horace more easily than some of the verses in *To a Louse: On Seeing One on a Lady's Bonnet at Church*—such a verse, for example, as:

> My sooth! right bauld ye set your nose out,
> As plump and grey as onie grozet;
> O for some rank, mercurial rozet,
>   Or fell, red smeddum,
> I'd gie you sic a hearty dose o't,
>   Wad dress your droddum!

I have urged them to read something simpler, like *To a Mouse: On Turning Her Up in her Nest with the Plough,* but even there they confess to an inability to understand such phrases as "a daimen icker in a thrave", "foggage green", and "cranreuch cauld". Perhaps someone will one day invent Basic Scots and translate Burns into it for the weaker brethren south of the Border. I am afraid, however, that in the course of the translation Burns's verse would lose nine-tenths of its magic.

'I myself was more or less brought up on Burns. At least, I spent my infancy in a nursery in which my nurse, during the intervals when she was not singing *The Protestant Boys* and *The Boyne Water,* used to croon *Ye Banks and Braes o' Bonnie Doon.* This was my first experience of disinterested melancholy. I did not know very clearly what the poem meant, but the lines:

> How can ye chant, ye little birds,
> And I sae weary fu' o' care?

made me feel pleasantly sad. And when I came to the close of the song with:

> And my fause lover stole my rose—
> But ah! he left the thorn wi' me—

I was initiated into the heartbreak at the heart of things. Thus I was fortunate enough to think of Burns from the beginning, not as a difficult, but as a simple and natural, writer . . .

'Burns was a popular poet in a sense in which no great English poet has been. Like Rudyard Kipling, he wrote verse that appealed to an enormous number of people who cared little for poetry in general. T. S. Eliot has praised Kipling as a very great verse-writer who occasionally became a poet, and Burns might be described as a great poet who was also a great verse-writer. And by verse I mean such lyrics as *A Man's a Man for a' That* and *My Wife's a Winsome Wee Thing*. Kipling, however, for all his genius, never became a writer for the people, appealing equally to the peer and the peasant. Burns is as likely to be quoted by a ploughman as by the Moderator of the Church of Scotland. He had, it must be admitted, the great advantage of having at hand some of the sweetest melodies on earth to which he set his verse. But other poets have had the same store of music to draw upon if they could have used it. Tom Moore in Ireland composed his verses to airs as lovely, but he never became a people's poet as Burns is a people's poet.

'He failed to do this because he was not, as Burns was, a representative man. Burns might be described as Everyman both in his strength and in his weakness. He was at once a sinner and a preacher, a singer of the heroic life and a celebrator of the easy-going joys of the tavern. He was torn by passions and repented of them. He was a pagan Puritan, as self-indulgent as Falstaff—and as likeable—but with a strain of the moralist in him that Falstaff lacked. The very variety of his nature put him on a footing with men of all sorts of conditions. He could express ideals—if you can call them ideals—of the village Lothario in *Anna of the Gowden Locks* and other poems, and at the same time in his *Epistle to a Young Friend* preach religion and morality more effectively than any minister of the Kirk.

'Burns has been taken to task for this "double life" that we find in his verse, and I have seen him accused of hypocrisy in his more virtuous utterances. Robert Louis Stevenson, if I remember right, described Burns's fits of remorse as "unmanly repentance". But surely the whole secret of Burns lies in the fact

MINIATURE BY ALEXANDER REID

that, like most human beings, he was compact of good and evil, and that he has expressed so many of the varying moods of fallible humanity with honesty and genius. Men have not been unknown who drink whisky to excess in what for the moment was a paradise of boon-companionship, and also gravely warned their nephews against following in their footsteps. Burns was human enough to want to see his nephews—if he had any—growing up to be better men than himself . . .'
[Here I am irresistibly reminded of dear Robert Lynd, whom I knew well, once saying to James Bone, the London editor of *The Manchester Guardian*, in a Fleet Street tavern: 'James, we are turning into the kind of men our fathers warned us against!']

'Some of Burns's songs have gone the round of the world—*My Love is like a Red, Red, Rose, Ae Fond Kiss*, and *Green Grow the Rashes, O* among them. Some of them owe a great deal to their musical setting; but others need no music to set off the magic of their verse. No love lyric more beautiful in its simplicity has been written since the Elizabethan Age than *The Silver Tassie*.

'And Burns felt more deeply than most of the Elizabethan lyrists. It is because his feeling was as profound as it was universal that he won the hearts as well as the literary enthusiasm of millions of human beings. His love of national freedom, his radicalism, became exalted into music as he wrote of them. His bitter hatred of hypocrisy, most powerfully expressed in *Holy Willie's Prayer*, sprang from the same passionate zeal for "the things that are most excellent".

'He was touched more deeply than common mortals are by the griefs as well as the joys that common mortals know; and in the last verses of *To a Mouse* his autobiography becomes the autobiography of a multitude:

> But, Mousie, thou art no thy lane,
> In proving foresight may be vain:
> The best-laid schemes o' mice and men
>   Gang aft a-gley,
> An' leave us nought but grief and pain,
>   For promis'd joy.

Still thou art blest, compar'd wi' me!
The present only toucheth thee;
But och! I backward cast my e'e
    On prospects drear,
An' forward, tho' I canna see,
    I guess an' fear!

Such lines, it may be thought, have become commonplace with repetition; but the very fact that so much of Burns has become commonplace and is still able to move us is a measure of his genius . . . He is certainly one of the most human, if not one of the greatest, poets—at his best, the minstrel, not only of a nation, but of mankind.'

For a last citation one goes to J. B. Priestley's highly authoritative *Literature and Western Man* and looks at the beginning of the chapter headed *The English Romantics* and reads:

' The "English" in the above title really refers to the language in which these romantic authors wrote, not to their nationality. True, most of them were English in both senses of the term, but not all. Indeed, Robert Burns, who cannot be ignored, was not only a Scot but also wrote almost all his best verse in a broad Scots dialect, almost a separate language. He is entirely an eighteenth-century figure, and stands outside the Romantic Movement, though there are romantic elements in his work.

He is very much of his country, which even today regards him affectionately as a national representative figure rather than as one of its authors. He passionately proclaims what almost every Scot, from lords at the head of ancient clans to peasant ploughmen, has thought and felt.

'The Scots are an odd people, more sharply divided than most between an austere piety and a rather grim devotion to knowledge, on the one side, and, on the other, a violent and reckless love of wine, woman and song, that no poet has celebrated more lustily than Burns, though he was equally capable of praising the industriousness, frugality and innocent family life of the opposite party. He was not concerned about having a fixed attitude and being consistent; he was a poet of

J. B. PRIESTLEY

the people, both the virtuous and the wicked, conscientious peasant proprietors and jolly beggars on the road, understood them all, having shared their lives, their toil and frugality and their debauchery; and it is all there, expressed with frankness and gusto, in his narrative poems and songs, especially in his songs, which have both satirical sharpness and lyrical beauty. Burns has the wide range of sympathy, the balance of classical and romantic elements, of a great poet, all the breadth if not (except to the Scots) all the height and depth; he might be described as one of the humbler and more limited master-singers.' Only the rabid Rabbie-ite will call this faint praise; it is, on the other hand, praise both fair and high.

Doubtless I shall be reproved for citing too many of other writers' opinions about Burns, familiar or recondite, and for not making my own estimate crystal-clear. The truth is that my own estimate, for what it is worth, is involved and *not* crystal-clear.

Burns as a poet was peculiarly unequal. At his very best he shines among the fifty or so poets who have immortalized themselves in the English language. Already I have stated my conviction that *Tam o' Shanter,* for sheer narrative drive and spontaneity and inevitability, has had nothing to equal it since Geoffrey Chaucer himself was writing. For piercing satire against canting churchmen it is hardly possible to mention, even within the eighteenth century, which was so hot on satire, anything so perfectly sustained as *Holy Willie's Prayer.* And for twenty or perhaps even thirty of his love songs Burns has—for once—not been overpraised. They are sweet and natural beyond sophistication; they are as ineffably fragrant as the old airs to which most of them were wedded (the poet himself often performing the ceremony, as it were).

The great body of Burns's verse, between the best and the worst, is marred by sentimentality—a tolerable fault, but one which is too often rendered quite intolerable by its insincerity. It is also, too often, quite careless technically—with slipshod and makeshift rhyming. The worst of his poetic output is doggerel, and unwitty doggerel at that—like the worst of Robert Herrick.

Yet this last poet at his best, that is in his handful of love lyrics, could be as good as the best of Burns—almost.

So much, in epitome and in sum, for Burns as a poet.

Burns as a human being I must freely allow to be fascinating to man or woman, bird or beast. To begin with, he *was* so human in both his virtues and his follies, his modesty and his immodesty, his pride and his conceit, his joy and his despair, his sustained flights and his sudden falls from grace. He was as incalculable as any poet who ever lived and loved. He would write a song to his Jean, the sturdy young woman he married, which can still make us cry with the noble sincerity of its sentiment, and the next day he can write a scurrilous letter about this same Jean to a boozing bosom-pal.

In judging such discrepancies and disparities of his we must ever remember that he was a poor and struggling eighteenth-century peasant by birth and upbringing. He had a natural dignity, and his behaviour with the gentry of Edinburgh was beyond criticism in its ease, reticence, and gallantry. But in his build and physical type—however he talked and worked—he was stocky, agricultural, of the soil, a sower and a reaper. He was also, very obviously, a dangerously attractive young man— with a curling mouth, a ready smile, and a glowing eye. It was not only the Ayrshire lasses who fell like ninepins. So, too, did the high-born dames as well as the sluts of the capital city. He was, in a word, irresistible, and there is hardly any evidence that he did any resisting. Like Mozart's Don Giovanni, as described by Leporello in the catalogue-song, he seems to have liked them in all shapes and sizes almost as much as they enjoyed him.

Yet here again we must recognise his utter frankness and his quite exceptional lack of hypocrisy in an age which stank and steamed with hypocrisy distinctly more than our own does. Burns loved love-making almost more than he loved verse-making, and he practised both arts with intensity and zeal and thoroughness. We turn yet again to the best of all judges of Burns in general—one means, of course, David Daiches, writing as recently as 1952—and we find this:

'Of the simple erotic folk-poems which Burns turned into charming and tender love-lyrics, it can be said only that Burns's transformation of them did not mean that he did not enjoy them in their original form or that he recognised an impassable barrier between the bawdy and the tenderly protective. *Burns saw this aspect of life steadily and saw it whole* [italics mine] as his letter to Richmond on the birth of twins makes clear. Part of the charm of such songs as "Oh, Wha My Babie Clouts Will Buy" derives from this combination of enjoyment of sex and its consequences. Burns did not have to deny or forget the physical aspects of sex in order to be able to rejoice in his fatherhoods or to write passionate love-songs, and there are indeed undertones of the purely physical in the most "respectable" of his love lyrics.'

That was the thing to say and it is said now—after one hundred and fifty years of blinking the facts, the facts of life as Robert Burns clearly saw them.

All this is not to deny a strong element of selfishness in the libertine—whether it be Don Giovanni or Robert Burns or, come to that, the Don's musical creator, Mozart, who himself enjoyed tavern-maids as well as countesses galore (as his letters when they are at length published in full are going to reveal). It is charming that Burns should take pride in his paternity and express this pride (as he several times did) in a lullaby of a lyric. But it is much less charming to think of the lengthy procession of impetuous and yielding young women paying for their few hours of pleasure with years of grief, worry, shame, and even destitution. No labour-pains, to name no other consequences, for the men! Let us think of that even while we chuckle over Professor Raleigh's witty parody regarding the annual celebration of the bard's birthday:

> For Scotland nane need droop or dwine;
> For them that feel their strength decline—
> The certain cure (it's just divine)
>   Each year returns.
> (What mony a lassie had lang syne)—
>   A nicht wi' Burns.

10 · Last Words

Finally, let me submit the text of two Burns orations which I have delivered in my time—but only in England as distinct from Scotland: one at Coventry, one at Beaconsfield, and both at Stratford-on-Avon (the first and the tenth Burns Dinners of the Warwickshire Caledonian Society).

AN ADDRESS TO A BURNS CLUB, JANUARY 1941

GENTLEMEN: This will not be the usual 'Burns Night', because I want, from this hazardous chair, to say some things that for too long have been left unsaid about your idol and demigod who was born on the 25th of January, 1759. I am extremely well aware of its being, for everybody but me, a comparatively unimportant detail that I was born on the 7th of January, 1905. But there is a certain significance, for me, in the fact that Robert Burns was born at Alloway in the Kyle section of Ayrshire, and that I was born in the Carrick section at Maybole, barely seven miles away. The circumstance helps me, in matters of upbringing and environment, to know what I am talking about, and to say something that I have wanted to say for about thirty years. Proudly I claim this unremarkable link with Burns—that I first saw the light in a town through which Tam o' Shanter must have passed, 'weel mounted on his grey mare Meg', on his way homeward to the village of Kirkoswald after Burns had finished telling his story.

Now, *Tam o' Shanter* is a great narrative poem—and 'great' is a word I never use loosely. There is good reason to suppose that it was Burns's own favourite among all his works. Carlyle, the poet's most biassed champion, rather oddly questions its power. But Carlyle in this, as in some other of his views on Burns, was wrong. Mrs. Carswell, who is on the whole the poet's best biographer to date, grants its supremacy. Professors Dixon and Grierson, in their anthology of longer English poems, say with justice that 'the narrative art of the poem is as great as Chaucer's, and between Chaucer and Burns comes no third'. Professor Hecht of Gottingen, author of the last first-rate book on Burns, says of this same work that 'above all the horrors of Hell there rises radiantly triumphant the incomparable humour of the poet, who in Tam o' Shanter has created a work in honour of his native place, that for power of inspiration and perfection of execution is worthy to stand beside the best tales in the literature of the world'.

There are only two qualifications to my complete agreement with those judgments. One is that the poet ought not to try to point a moral when the poem has none. It concludes:

> Now, wha this tale o' truth shall read,
> Ilk man and mother's son take heed;
> Whene'er to drink you are inclin'd,
> Or cutty-sarks rin in your mind,
> Think! ye may buy the joys o'er dear;
> Remember Tam o' Shanter's mare.

But what had poor Meg to do with Tam's insobriety and rashness? And why was it not Tam himself who sustained the loss, say, of at least his 'gude blue bonnet'? Why has the mare to pay for the master's folly? My one other objection is that the poem, to the lay reader, is almost as hard to follow as the archaic Chaucer himself. Every edition of Burns should, in my view, have a definition of all dialect words given in a footnote to the page on which they occur. Every edition that I know

contents itself with a glossary at the end of the volume, which
seems to say: 'The English may apply here if they must.' The
truth of the whole matter is that Burns was at his best only when
he wrote in the eighteenth-century Ayrshire dialect, and this
dialect today is often obscure not only to English but also to
Scottish and even to Ayrshire readers. I know well that the
Scots do not care to admit this difficulty. But there it is, never-
theless. Take as a perfectly fair example the first few lines of
Tam o' Shanter itself:

> When chapman billies leave the street,
> And drouthy neibors neibors meet,
> As market-days are wearing late,
> An' folk begin to tak the gate;
> While we sit bousing at the nappy,
> An' getting fou and unco happy,
> We think na on the lang Scots miles,
> The mosses, waters, slaps, and styles,
> That lie between us and our hame . . .

In my estimation there are in these nine lines no fewer than
seven or possibly eight words which the non-Scottish poetry
reader cannot be expected to understand without a glossary,
and I do hereby challenge any average Scot attending to me
now to say offhand, and without hesitation or consultation, what
are 'chapman billies', whether 'take the gate' means 'go home'
or 'lock up for the night', whether 'nappy' signifies a drink or a
tavern, and what exactly is a 'slap'. If I were, really and truly,
delivering this Address to an actual Burns club in my native
country, I should be much surprised if straight and accurate
answers were immediately forthcoming to any of these questions.

My reasonable 'sma' request' is that, at these annual celebra-
tions of his birthday, this remarkable man and poet should be
studied more and worshipped less. My countrymen rave more
than they read. I have always been particularly 'scunnert' or
nauseated—and so, too, would Burns, to give him his due—at
his being so often held up on these occasions as not only the
single Scottish poet of note (to say nothing of the inconsiderable

clutter of English songsters led, presumably, by Shakespeare), but also as the very pattern of honest manliness apart from his song-making. Burns had many failings and freely confessed them. Among other things, he was as lecherous as a stoat. He treated his loves, the mothers of some of his children, abominably; and Jean Armour, whom he eventually married after she had borne him two sets of twins, showed perception as well as tolerance when she exclaimed, even while adopting yet another of his stray offspring: 'Oor Robin should hae had twa wives!'

Yet with all his imperfections he was, it is clear, irresistible as a person, and this fascination survives. He can charm even the severest of his biographers. Thus Mrs. Carswell has confessed: 'He must have been a personable young man. He had a large, dark head and a dark but fresh complexion, arched glowing eyes, an upturned nose, and a curly mouth. It was a face that easily changed from a sombre and even forbidding thoughtfulness to a sparkling impudence or a persuasive ardour.'

And his contemporary, Josiah Walker, has this notable statement: 'In no man is sexuality more powerful or apparent. The presence of women produces an instant revolution in his manner. The tone of his conversation and demeanour changes and he endeavours to recommend himself by other powers of pleasing. Nor are those powers employed without success, even with those who could not for a moment admit a thought of him as a lover.'

Dozens of estimates like these, both new and old, prove what an attractive and pardonable person Robert was. His shining likeableness radiates even the more erratic stretches of his verse, and even the self-conscious phrasing of his prose and his letters. But all I maintain, and insist on maintaining, is that this likeableness should not blind us wholly to the faults and inequalities of his verse. Enough has already been said of his one great narrative poem. As a satirist he is also superb, being fifth only to Pope, Swift, Dryden, and Byron. In *The Jolly Beggars* he provides a saturnalia of unexampled gusto. The darkness of the dialect of other long poems like *Hallowe'en* has undoubtedly some lightning-flashes of genius. There is a rich amount of humour in several of the *Epistles*. There is a justly praised, and for once not overpraised, humanity, simplicity, and wisdom in the famous poems addressed to a mouse and a mountain daisy. And, like many greater and profounder poets, he wrote a deal of sorry stuff!

Lastly, for the famous Songs. When, the other day, I pointed out to an eminent Scot that of the four lines which begin one of Burns's best-known songs:

> O my love's like a red, red rose
>   That's newly sprung in June:
> O my love's like the melodie
>   That's sweetly played in tune . . .

the second line is fairly bad and the fourth rank bad to anyone with an ear or a taste for verse, he gazed at me with gasping stupefaction, walked away, and has avoided me ever since. Were I to express this view in public the whole of Caledonia would be stern and wild and unreasonable, and would heed me not at all when I went on to say that the first and third lines have a magical, natural beauty, and that the whole of the rest of the song is flawless perfection. Some eighteen to twenty of the songs inspired by love, and one or two of those inspired by drink, are not less magical and not less flawlessly perfect:

> O Willie brew'd a peck o' maut,
>   And Rob and Allan cam to pree;
> Three blyther hearts that lee-lang nicht,
>   Ye wad na find in Christendie.
>
> We are na fou, we're nae that fou,
>   But just a drappie in our e'e;
> The cock may craw, the day may daw,
>   And aye we'll taste the barley bree.
>
> Here are we met, three merry boys,
>   Three merry boys, I trow, are we;
> And monie a night we've merry been,
>   And monie mae we hope to be!

It is the moon, I ken her horn,
    That's blinkin' in the lift sae hie;
She shines sae bright to wyle us hame,
    But, by my sooth! she'll wait a wee!

Wha first shall rise to gang awa,
    A cuckold, coward loon is he!
Wha last beside his chair shall fa',
    He is the King amang us three!

Things like the serenade to Mary Morison seem not to have been made; they have grown like wild flowers. They glisten like a spring morning in the Galloway hills. They sing themselves, even if you do not happen to know the lovely old tunes to which they are often so happily wedded. They are the cream of Burns's life-work, and into them he put all the art he had, and most of his heart as well.

There is a valuable letter—No. 586 in the authoritative De Lancey Ferguson edition—which gives us details of Burns's method of composing these songs:

'When I feel my Muse beginning to jade, I retire to the solitary fireside of my study, and there commit my effusions to paper; swinging, at intervals, on the hind-legs of my elbow chair, by way of calling forth on my own critical strictures, as my pen goes on . . .'

In the mind's eye I see Rabbie across the years, still swinging in his chair, and with a grin for the critical strictures of chiels like me, serene in the knowledge that *Tam o' Shanter* is sheer genius and that a handful of songs like *Ca' the Yowes* and *Ye Banks and Braes* and *O, wert thou in the Cauld Blast* are among the supreme love lyrics in English, Scottish, or any other language of the world.

A DISSERTATION ON ROBERT BURNS, 1943

ON January 25th, wherever Scotsmen are all over the world, and throughout my native land, and most especially in every little town and little village in my native Ayrshire—they will once again be celebrating the birth of Robert Burns. 'Drouthy neibors neibors meet' as the poet himself says—'drouthy' meaning 'thirsty'—and suppers are eaten and washed down, and toasts drunk (especially one to 'The Immortal Memory') and the same glowing platitudes are uttered year after year, and a great time is had by all.

'Who is this Bobby Burns?' said a great English nobleman at a public banquet some years ago. And Auld Scotia—which is inclined to lose its sense of humour especially where its first poet and his reputation are concerned—rose up in its wrath, failed to see the noble lord was ponderously joking, poured contempt upon his noble ignorance in its newspapers, and said that at the very least he might be told that the poet could be familiarly referred to as 'Rabbie' but never as 'Bobby'. Very much as you must always say 'Scots' (or so they protest) and never, never, never Scotch—with the curious exceptions of Scotch mist, Scotch broth, Scotch shortbread, butterscotch, and—of course— Scotch whisky. Hoots awa and clishmaclaver! . . . .

Anyhow this great Scotchman—a truly great Scotchman he was—was born at Alloway in Ayrshire, son of a poor crofter, in the year 1759 and on January 25th. He was not at all badly educated—as a peasant's education went in those days. He had the urge to learn—which is three-quarters of the battle; and good luck in his choice of village schoolmasters brought him acquaintance with the English poets whom he first admired and then began to emulate and imitate.

But the grinding need of earning a living left him little enough time for reading or writing. He worked hard and (being a poet with a poet's typical temperament) he played hard as well. He moved to one bare upland Ayrshire farm after another. He ploughed and he poetised. It is all very romantic and very touching, but it was never very practical. You cannot make a real success of a ploughed field if you are meditating an address to a mouse whose nest you have just laid in ruins, or another to a daisy, a mountain daisy, whose tender brown-pink stalk you have just had to sever in two. Burns wrote his poems instead of following his plough to the end of the furrow. The good earth's loss was the wide world's gain.

Burns' father died in the year 1784, and left him to try farming for himself. In the following year—when he was twenty-five or twenty-six—he wrote some of his most famous poems— *The Jolly Beggars, The Twa Herds, The Epistle to Davy, Death and Dr. Hornbrook, Hallowe'en, The Cotter's Saturday Night, The Holy Fair, Holy Willie's Prayer,* and *The Address to a Mouse.* One of his biographers justly says that if we had only the verses of that year, Burns would be known as a great poet. But being a Scotch biographer he indulges in the usual uncritical over-statement with regard to Burns, and says that on the strength of the products of this year Burns 'remains the greatest of known popular poets'! Certain it is that the works I have just mentioned give us Burns's full force in satire, in jollity, in domestic pathos, in wit, in tenderness, in humanity and brother-love, and in that crusade against cant and sanctimony on which he spent almost too much of his spiritual energy.

In the following year, while still continuing to write at his best and living at the very peak—both in spirit and in the flesh— he first published his poems. This was the famous and now much-sought-after Kilmarnock Edition of only six hundred copies. He had been on the verge of a voyage to Jamaica to escape from a wild mixture of poverty and amorous entanglements. But the praise with which his book was hailed, and the promise of fame and prosperity that its immediate success held out, kept him in Scotland after all. In the winter he went to Edinburgh and found himself a lion—the cynosure of all eyes— the toast of fair women and witty and scholarly men. The experience might have turned the head of many an even stronger-willed fellow. But Rabbie behaved, on the whole, extremely well in these intoxicating circumstances. We may gather his pride and good sense from his own words, in his own Journal and Letters for this period:

'I am entering the lists flushed with hope to struggle for notice, for distinction, in common with hundreds of others. But who are they? Men like myself. And seven-tenths of them come short of my natural advantages! Besides I have two good pairs of breeks. My coat is Scotch of the best. And I have a Holland cravat, stockings and pumps. That no scheme to frustrate my hopes may prosper is the prayer of Robert Burns.

There's a youth in this city, it were a great pity
That he from our lassies should wander awa',
For he's bonie and braw, weel favor'd with a',
And his hair has a natural buckle and a'.

His coat is the hue o' his bonnet sae blue
His fecket is white as the new driven snaw,
His hose they are blue and his shoon like the sloe
And his clean siller-buckles, they dazzle us a'.

My Highland bonnet, once my proudest dress, is at present exchanged for a ten shilling *hat*. So hey brave Robin lad, cock up your beaver!'

A good natural conceit of himself, you see! He wouldn't have been a Scot without it. Burns had charm and knew it. We may gather from other private letters and memoirs of the period how admirably he behaved in Edinburgh in spite of all the giddy flattery. Thus a fashionable Mrs. Alison Cockburn writes to a friend: 'The town is a present agog with the ploughman poet, who receives adulation with native dignity and is the very figure of his profession, strong and coarse, but he has a most enthusiastic heart. The man will be spoiled, if he can spoil, but he keeps his simple manners and is quite sober.' And another patron and observer, Professor Dalziel, writes to a friend of his: 'We have got a poet in town just now, whom everybody is taking notice of—a ploughman from Ayrshire—a man of unquestionable genius. He is a fellow of strong common sense. But he runs the risk of being spoiled by the excessive attention paid him just now by persons of all ranks. I saw him at an assembly t' other night. The Duchess of Gordon and other ladies of rank took notice of him. He behaves wonderfully well, very independent, though not forward.' In that last sentence is the clue to Burns's successful decorum in Edinburgh—it is a hint for the successful behaviour of all persons lacking good birth and education. It is only another way of saying what Logan Pearsall Smith has told us his tutor said to him as a child: 'It is most important in this world to be pushing but—it is fatal to seem so!' Burns was not the man to make that kind of mistake.

In 1787 the poems were reprinted, and the result saved him for some time from any further financial embarrassment. In the following year he married Jean Armour, a pleasant sensible woman who had already borne him two sets of twins! The other

THE DUCHESS OF GORDON'S ASSEMBLY

year I visited the little house in Mauchline which Burns occupied
with Jean some time before this belated marriage. A grim old
Scotch-woman showed me round the well-kept little museum.
'Here's the room occupied by Burns and Jean Armour in the
year 1785.' 'But surely,' said I, seriously and without a smile,
'the marriage didn't take place till 1788?' The old girl gazed
at me grimly for a second or two and then repeated: 'I'm only
here to say that this is the room occupied by Burns and Jean
Armour in the year 1785. *And that's the bed!*' So I crossed the
room and reverently patted the bed, and the incident was
closed.

Burns's character is a most extraordinary mixture of the
admirable and the deplorable. He was strongly over-sexed and
he broke many hearts. He could be careless and even supremely
selfish in his love-making. Beautiful and tender love-lyrics may
or may not compensate for his libertinism—it wholly depends on
the reader's point of view. The age-old argument about morality
and the artist is peculiarly pronounced in Burns's case. A
striking instance occurs in his own Journal where we find Burns
talking about his wife in a positively bumptious, complacent
way: and then suddenly the overbearing prose turns into
exquisite verse when a famous lyric then and there falls from
his pen—a love-lyric addressed to his own wife during the
honeymoon. Here is the passage:

'Once much lov'd (I lov'd her to distraction) and still loved,
my girl has been doubly kinder to me than even the best of
women. Of the four children she bore me in seventeen months,
two sets of twins, my eldest boy only is living. But I reckon on
twelve brace of children against I celebrate my twelfth wedding-
day—twenty-four useful members of society! I am so enamoured
of her prolific twin-bearing mint that I have given her the legal
title which I now avow to the world. *I intend to present Mrs. Burns
with a printed shawl.* [Italics my own.]

. . . I am pleased with my conduct and really more and more
pleased with my choice. If I have not got polite tattle, modish
manners and fashionable dress, I *have* got a clean-limbed
bewitching young hussey with the soundest constitution, the

most placid good nature, the sweetest temper, vigorous health, and sprightly cheerfulness set off to the best advantage by a more than common handsome figure and a warm heart.' The following day has this entry: 'I have just put the last hand to a song and I think I may say of it "here is a work of mine finished in my very finest style" . . .'

TO JEAN

O my love is like a red red rose
That's newly sprung in June.
O my love is like a melodie
That's sweetly played in tune.

As fair art thou, my bonie lass,
So deep in love am I,
And I will love thee still, my dear,
Till a' the seas gang dry.

Till a' the seas gang dry, my dear,
And the rocks melt wi' the sun!
And I will love thee still, my dear,
While the sands o' life shall run.

And fare thee weel, my only love,
And fare thee weel, a while,
And I will come again, my love,
Tho' it were ten thousand mile.

Dated the very same day, there is extant a letter from Burns to his friend Robert Ainslie. It runs: 'My dear Friend—Almost my first welcome to this place was the enclosed letter [from one May Cameron, an Edinburgh servant-girl, saying she was out of a job, destitute, and about to bear an infant]. Please call and send for the wench and give her ten or twelve shillings . . . Advise her out to some country friends . . . I am very sorry for this, but what is done is done.'

What are we to make of this man—this singular mixture of heart and heartlessness, of Christian morality and pagan immorality, of conscience and caddishness, of sober sense and insobriety? The truth is that Rabbie was even more of a mixie-maxie than most other great poets, lesser and greater. He was both strong and weak, powerful and feckless, firm and inconstant, fickle and loyal, good and bad. He suffered occasionally from remorse for all his sins and follies—but even that emotion was mixed up inextricably with nervous depression and a strong tendency to hypochondria.

He died, prematurely worn out, at the age of thirty-seven in the year 1796. Distinguished doctors—Scottish I need hardly say —have written books and treatises to prove that Burns's death was due to rheumatic fever and not as the direct result of prolonged self-indulgence in various directions. They may convince others; they do not convince me.

What I most admire about Burns the man was his honest lack of humbug. He knew about his weaknesses and admitted them— far more than his idolaters do today! He was perfectly frank throughout his lifework about his love of strong drink and of 'dear deluding woman, the joy of joys'. And what I admire most about Burns the poet are the remarkable poems already mentioned— the exquisite love-songs like the serenade to Mary Morison:

> O Mary, at thy window be,
> It is the wish'd, the tryst'd hour!
> Those smiles and glances let me see,
> That make the miser's treasure poor;
> How blythely would I bide the stoure,
> A weary slave frae sun to sun,
> Could I the rich reward secure,
> The lovely Mary Morison.
>
> Yestreen when to the trembling string
> The dance gaed through the lichted ha'
> To thee my fancy took its wing,
> I sat, but neither heard nor saw;
> Tho' this was fair, and that was braw,
> And yon the toast o' a' the town,
> I sigh'd, and said among them a',
> 'Ye are na Mary Morison'. . .

And most of all, the splendid breathless narrative poem of *Tam o' Shanter*, full of fun and fright and colour and dramatic vivacity. Laying my hand on my critical heart I declare this to be the finest narrative poem since the days of Geoffrey Chaucer. This is the highest critical praise. Yet each and all of my countrymen, lost in admiration of their idol, and reading no one else's poetry whatsoever (least of all trying to read *The Canterbury Tales*) would undoubtedly say, if they heard me: 'And who's your Geoffrey Chaucer when he's at home?'

This, in conclusion, I will say—and it may, of course, be the Scot, the Ayrshireman, in me that makes me say it!—that *Tam o' Shanter* has, within six of its lines, the best description in literature of a wild wet thunderstorm:

> The wind blew as 'twad blawn its last;
> The rattling showers rose on the blast;
> The speedy gleams the darkness swallow'd;
> Loud, deep, and lang the thunder bellow'd
> That night, a child might understand,
> The Deil had business on his hand.

There's the truly great Robert Burns, strong, vivid, and sure of himself. There are times—there are moments—when we cease to wonder why the entire Scottish nation should be so besotted about him.

Index

STIRLING
DISTRICT
LIBRARY